THE ADKINS SITE:
A PALAEO-INDIAN HABITATION
AND ASSOCIATED STONE STRUCTURE

by Richard Michael Gramly
Curator of Anthropology
Buffalo Museum of Science

With a Preface by:

Peter L. Storck
Curator
Department of New World Archaeology
Royal Ontario Museum

Persimmon Press Monographs in Archaeology, 1988

To My Friends in the Maine Warden Service
for Their Many Kindnesses

Library of Congress Cataloguing-in-Publication Data

Gramly, Richard Michael
    The Adkins site.
    (Persimmon Press monographs in archaeology)
    Bibliography: p.
    Includes index.
    1. Adkins Site (Maine). 2. Paleo-Indians—Maine—Antiquities. 3. Excavations (Archaeology)—Maine. 4. Maine—Antiquities. I. title. II. Series.
E78.M2G695   1988   974.1'01   87-32822
ISBN 0-9615462-2-0 (pbk.)

Cover illustration: View across the Adkins site looking to the northwest at time of low lake level, October, 1984; excavated stone structure in foreground.

Printed by Partners' Press, Kenmore Ave., Buffalo, N.Y. 14217.

CONTENTS

ACKNOWLEDGEMENTS

The discovery and exploration of the Adkins site stem from financial assistance provided by the Maine Historic Preservation Commission, Augusta, Maine. Their funding and support of archaeological reconnaissances in western Maine have resulted in studies of several Palaeo-Indian encampments threatened with destruction by erosion. These public monies were matched by contributions from the Buffalo Museum of Science, Buffalo, New York, and by the labor and donations of volunteer archaeologists — both amateur and professional. The Maine State Museum also contributed to our work at the Adkins site.

The Maine State Museum, the Maine Warden Service, and the Maine National Guard cooperated in the airlifting and removal to Augusta of the Adkins stone structure. I am deeply grateful for their help in preserving this rare monument of the Palaeo-Indian era as part of the exhibit "Twelve Thousand Years in Maine."

The list of volunteer excavators who explored the Adkins site is topped by Charles Adkins for whom the site is named. Alexandra Morss, an employee of the expedition, worked longer hours than were expected of her, and to her diligence and Charlie's keen eyes we owe the discovery of the ancient encampment.

I wish to thank the following colleagues for their time and labor: John Aures, Dr. Bruce Bourque and his students from Bates College, Zygmunt Bieniulis, Wynn Bowers, C. D. Cox, Jim Fell, Garry Forger, Stefana Paskoff, Junior Poor, Dr. Arthur Spiess, Deborah Brush Wilson, and Susan Woodward.

Mrs. Annie Perkins of Kennebunk, Maine, very kindly placed her cabin on Aziscohos Lake at our disposal, which was a boon to both excavators and visitors.

I am indebted to Manuel dos Passos for supplying the excellent photograph on the back cover of this monograph.

PREFACE

This book on the Adkins site is the second major study of Early Paleo-Indian material to come from Dr. Gramly's long-term project in the Magalloway River valley in northwestern Maine. The "Magalloway valley project" might be said to have started in 1979 with the discovery of the Vail site and since that time Dr. Gramly has conducted field work almost yearly in the region leading to the discovery of over half a dozen Early Paleo-Indian sites (Vail occupation; Vail kill sites 1, 1980, and 2, 1983; Adkins, 1984; Lower and Upper Wheeler Dam, 1985/86; and Cox, 1985) and an important chert source (Ledge Ridge, 1980). The 1982 report on the Vail site (published as Volume 30 of the *Bulletin of the Buffalo Society of Natural Sciences*) was Dr. Gramly's first comprehensive report on his Magalloway valley work and its appearance initiated what promised to be a series of publications on his discoveries. This study on the Adkins site is in essence the second volume of that publication series. As a highly readable — indeed provocative — mix of "plain language" archaeological analysis (Chapters 1-5) and historical fiction (part of Chapter 6) it confirms the promise that many significant publications will be forthcoming from a very productive survey and excavation project that is currently in its ninth year — and continuing.

The Adkins site is small, covering an area of approximately 72 square metres, and produced only 2 fluted points (one of which is incomplete) and 415 other artifacts and flakes. However, the site is disproportionately significant for its size because of its physical setting, the distribution patterns of the artifact material, and the presence of a nearby stone structure composed of large boulders. With respect to its setting in the landscape, Gramly notes that the Adkins site occurs, as do all of the other occupation sites he has discovered, on the eastern margin of the valley. He speculates, plausibly I believe, that the locations were intentionally selected by Early Paleo-Indian hunters to be downwind of animal movements. The small sample of 417 artifacts and flakes occurs in four discrete yet related patterns which Gramly believes were the product of a single occupation in a skin-covered structure. Thus, the artifacts may reflect something of Early Paleo-Indian social organization as it relates to the movements (perhaps seasonal in nature) of individual or allied families across the landscape. One of the most intriguing "artifact" patterns is the occurrence near the presumed tent structure of an oval grouping of heavy boulders each weighing 100 kilograms or more. These boulders enclose an area about 3 metres in diameters and may represent, Gramly argues, a permanent cache for meat storage. The notion that Early Paleo-Indian peoples may have used storage caches as part of their overall subsistence strategy has recently taken on greater interest in Early Man studies. In a paper published in 1982, for example, an archaeologist in western North America, George Frison, reviewed the evidence for Early Paleo-Indian meat storage caches on the Northern Plains (see also Frison and Todd 1986) and argued that they were essential to winter survival in that region. It gives one pause to suppose that a similar, perhaps related, cultural pattern of behaviour was practiced by Early Paleo-Indian peoples 3000 kilometers to the east in the Magalloway valley. One is reminded of other arguments suggesting that the Early Paleo-Indian occupation of North America was accomplished by the spread of a single people and cultural tradition. Be that as it may, the presence of a possible meat storage cache at the Adkins site, soon to be on display at the Maine State Museum in Augusta, should do much to stimulate research on Early Paleo-Indian caches — whether consisting of meat, artifacts, or raw material — and their possible role in subsistence and other related activities.

For the specialist in Early Paleo-Indian studies and the interested lay person generally, this book presents much important data and interpretation on several contemporary themes in Early Man research: site location strategy, patterns of chert utilization and the direction of band movements, social organization, lithic technology as related to raw material type, and subsistence patterns. In addition to this, however, the book is a pleasure to read. The narrative style of writing involves the reader in the process of discovery as lived by Dr. Gramly both in the field and in the laboratory and it is difficult not to share his enthusiasm in his work and his sense of wonder as to what it was like to live in the late Ice Age landscape of northern Maine. Although it is not possible to actually go back into the glacial "age of discovery" of our ancestors, this study brings us a step closer and opens yet other doors in our mental journey to that most wondrous time.

References Cited

Frison, George C.
    1982   Paleo-Indian winter subsistence strategies on the High Plains. *In* Plains Indian Studies: A Collection of Essays in Honor of John C. Ewers and Waldo R. Wedel, D. H. Ubelaker and H. J. Viola (eds.). *Smithsonian Contributions to Anthropology* No. 30. Washington D.C.
Frison, George C. and Lawrence C. Todd
    1986   *The Colby Mammoth Site: Taphonomy and Archaeology of A Clovis Kill in Northern Wyoming.* University of New Mexico Press, Albuquerque.
Gramly, Richard Michael
    1982   The Vail Site: A Palaeo-Indian Encampment in Maine. *Bulletin of the Buffalo Society of Natural Sciences* 30. Buffalo, New York.

P. L. Storck
Department of New World Archaeology
Royal Ontario Museum
100 Queen's Park
Toronto, Ontario, Canada

November, 1987

List of Tables

List of Figures

List of Plates

THE ADKINS SITE

*"But lo! here comes a Frank from many days journey off, and he walks up
to the very place, and . . . Here, says he, is the palace; there, says he, is
the gate; and he shows us what has been all our lives beneath our feet,
without our having known anything about it. Wonderful! wonderful! Is it
by books, is it by magic, is it by your prophets, that you have learnt these
things? Speak, O Bey; tell me the secret of wisdom."*

Austen Henry Layard. *Nineveh and Its Remains*
(Vol. 2): 71. 1858.

The History of Archaeological Research in the Magalloway River Valley

A visit to the Vail Palaeo-Indian site on the eastern shore of Aziscohos Lake in
July, 1979, marked the beginning of archaeological research in the Magalloway River
valley, northwestern Maine. Until that time no archaeologist had explored the river
from its headwaters on the Quebec border to its mouth 65 kilometers south on Umbagog Lake.

In 1951 Howard Sargent conducted excavations at Molls Rock on Umbagog Lake
within a short distance of the mouth of the Magalloway River (Gramly and Rutledge
1982: 124). Warren K. Moorehead and his team of exploring excavators from the R.
S. Peabody Foundation, Andover, Massachusetts, stopped at promising locations in
southern Oxford County, Maine and adjacent parts of New Hampshire during the 1920's
(Moorehead 1922, 1931); however, there is no record that they searched for prehistoric
sites in extreme northwestern Maine in the neighborhood of Aziscohos Lake.

Exploration of the Vail site in the upper Magalloway valley took place sporadical-
ly from September, 1979, until October 1980. During this period of directed activity,
there were few opportunities to reconnoitre the surrounding countryside. Nevertheless,
on a few occasions it was possible to conduct brief surveys with the help of Maine game
wardens, Charles Adkins, Eric Wight and Tom Jacobs. Chert outcrops at Ledge Ridge,
22 kilometers north of the Vail site, were inspected. As a result of this discovery, it
is now known that a great deal of stone used by Palaeo-Indian knappers of the
Magalloway valley was derived from this source (Gramly 1985a: 76).

Also in 1980, Vail kill site #1 was discovered 200 m west of the habitation site at
a location normally inundated by the waters of man-made Aziscohos Lake (Gramly
1982: 14). The implication of this find was immediately apparent, *viz.,* the entire
37-kilometer stretch of Aziscohos lakebed likely harbored prehistoric sites. At every
lowering of lake level it became necessary to search for artifacts. During rare periods
when the waters dropped five meters or more, the meandering, almost tortuous, channel of the Magalloway River would be exposed. Over time we learned that small archaeological sites dotted the banks of the modern river and that there were other, older
sites along anciently abandoned channels. Palaeo-Indian remains seemed to be confined to glacial outwash plains elevated 5-10 meters above the present river; on the
other hand, late prehistoric Ceramic Period sites as well as nineteenth century loggers' camps were located at the river's edge.

At a time of low lake level in October, 1982, the writer and colleagues from the Maine State Museum, the Maine Historic Preservation Commission, McGill University and the University of Montreal revisited the Vail site in order to complete the investigation of Locus A — a dwelling site. Vail kill site #1 and environs were inspected for Palaeo-Indian artifacts that might have been uncovered by wind, waves and rain, but nothing of importance was found.

In fall, 1983, discoveries of two fragmentary fluted points by cottagers at Aziscohos Lake prompted Arthur Spiess and the writer to search the bare lakebed to the northwest of the Vail encampment. These visits resulted in the identification of Vail kill site #2, approximately 750 m upwind from the Palaeo-Indian habitations (Gramly 1984a).

A rumor that Aziscohos Lake would be drained for repairing the dam at the Falls of the Magalloway in summer or fall, 1984, prompted the hiring of watchers to monitor the lake level and to collect artifacts. This precaution was justified and all expenditures handsomely repaid by the discovery of 14 prehistoric stations (Gramly 1985b). At least four of these sites proved to be Palaeo-Indian in age. One of them was named the Adkins site after its discoverer, Warden Charles Adkins of Rangeley, Maine. Warden E. Wight gave his name to a second site.

Emergency funding for mapping the new sites and for salvage excavations or test-pits was obtained from the Maine Historic Preservation Commission and the Buffalo Museum of Science. A small crew was hired and with the help of volunteers the Adkins and Wight sites were laid bare. Additional digging was undertaken at the Vail kill sites #1 and #2 and at the Vail encampment itself. At kill site #1 a rare Palaeo-Indian Plano projectile point was unearthed (Doyle *et al.* 1985: 16, 32).

As a result of six weeks of steady labor, several thousand Palaeo-Indian artifacts were recovered. Using power machinery for test-trenching, deeply sedimented sections of the Vail site were probed and samples for radiocarbon dating were collected by C. Vance Haynes, who was a guest of the expedition for a few days.

In late October, 1984, after a period of unexpectedly warm temperatures and clear skies, weather conditions deteriorated and excavation was brought to a halt. Racing against the onset of winter freeze-up, arrangements were made to dismantle and remove an important ancient stone structure at the Adkins site. With the help of the Maine National Guard and local volunteers, staff of the Maine State Museum air-lifted the structure by helicopter to a storage area at Aziscohos Dam. From there it was transported by trailer to Augusta, Maine.

In May, 1985, the writer and friends from New York and Maine returned to Aziscohos Lake in order to continue exploring prehistoric sites discovered the preceding year. A few more days of work were devoted to the Adkins site, and spoil earth from the 1984 excavation was resieved with a very fine mesh in hopes of gleaning small tool fragments and debitage that had been overlooked. The primary focus of the 1985 fieldwork was, however, the Morss Palaeo-Indian encampment lying approximately two kilometers northeast of Vail.

Three weeks of digging at Morss netted over 500 artifacts that were distributed among three habitation loci. It was established that Morss was a closed site, totally free of more recent cultural remains. The discoveries at Morss will be the subject of a future monograph.

In 1984 and 1985 several reconnaissances were carried out in the neighborhood of Ledge Ridge, Parmachenee Lake and tributaries of the upper Magalloway River.

Explorations in this densely forested region yielded no *bona-fide* Palaeo-Indian artifacts, although evidence of ancient quarrying at Ledge Ridge, possibly of the Palaeo-Indian era, was noted (Gramly 1985b).

Two summertime visits to Aziscohos Lake in 1985 were rewarded with finding a pair of badly eroded Palaeo-Indian encampments at the extreme northern end of the lake. These stations, known as Lower Wheeler Dam and Upper Wheeler Dam, were explored as completely as time and manpower permitted. Work at both sites was not concluded until August, 1986. Fieldwork was abetted by Bruce Bourque and other personnel of the Maine State Museum who were complemented by a team of amateur archaeologists from New York, Maine and Ohio.

Late in 1985 at the onset of bitter weather another visit was made to Aziscohos Lake. The eastern shore between the Morss and Adkins sites was methodically inspected. The exposed lakebed west of the Vail site was also scanned. A thin scatter of flaked stone artifacts situated mid-way between the Vail and Adkins sites, first noted in 1984, was reexamined. Our suspicions that this station was Palaeo-Indian in age were confirmed with the discovery of a channel flake and other debris from fluted point manufacture. The locality was designated the Cox site, after C. D. Cox — a dedicated amateur archaeologist and veteran of numerous expeditions to Palaeo-Indian sites in Maine, Tennessee and New York.

The 1986 field season in the Magalloway valley was iniated with another visit to Ledge Ridge. Systematic examination of the mountain's southeastern flank turned up an outcrop of banded maroon and tan chert, identical in appearance and texture to some artifacts at the Cox site. This find was welcome confirmation of the belief, first stated in 1982, that Ledge Ridge was an important resource of Palaeo-Indian toolmakers.

Later that same year the writer and volunteer excavators returned to the sites at Wheeler Dam in order to map them and to finish exploratory test-pitting. As our schedule permitted, reconnaissance along the Little Magalloway River and northwest arm of Aziscohos Lake was pursued. No new Palaeo-Indian sites were met, although artifacts of more recent periods were collected.

In September, 1987, at the end of summer drought and lowered lake level another visit was paid to the Adkins and Cox sites. A small spread of forest soil containing Palaeo-Indian stone artifacts, which was unfortunately overlooked during earlier investigations at Adkins, was laid bare. The entire excavation was then rescraped in search of other specimens, but little was discovered. The Cox site was also staked out and explored, and two small loci that marked work stations of Palaeo-Indian stone knappers were identified.

All artifacts discovered in the Magalloway valley since 1979, amounting to at least 15,000 specimens, have been catalogued. They are curated at the Maine State Museum, the Buffalo Museum of Science or in private collections throughout northern New England. The majority of objects, perhaps 97%, are held by these two museums and are accessible to scholars.

Since 1979, nearly nine months of excavations have taken place on sites around Aziscohos Lake. During eight years of archaeological research, at least 13 separate reconnaissances, each lasting 2-5 days, have been carried out upstream of the Falls of the Magalloway. By comparison, little attention has been given to the valley south of the Falls downriver to Umbagog Lake. Undoubtedly prehistoric sites await discovery there, but vegetation is dense and exposure is poor, making searches difficult.

The Adkins site belongs to a cluster of at least 24 prehistoric sites on record for the upper Magalloway River valley north of the Falls. Eight of these sites were occupied by Palaeo-Indians; none of the eight was inhabited at a later period.

On the face of it, it appears that Palaeo-Indian sites are perched high above the modern Magalloway River while Neo-Indian stations cluster nearer the present river-bank. This impression of patterning across the valley scape is unverifiable by systematic archaeological survey due to the unpredictable and fluctuating level of Aziscohos Lake. With such an unsatisfactory, and possibly biased, understanding of the valley's archaeological record, it is difficult to judge the role and importance of the Adkins site in respect to other occupations. Any reconstruction of human behavior in the valley over long periods or phases is necessarily provisional and subject to rethinking as new data are gathered. Only basic facts about the Adkins site and assemblage are likely to weather unscathed future enquiries and new investigations.

Physical and Cultural Setting
of the Adkins Site

The Adkins site lies on the eastern shore of Aziscohos Lake, Parkertown Township, northern Oxford County at an altitude of 465 meters (1,513 feet) above sea level. Its geodetic position is Latitude 45°01'49" N., Longitude 71°00'15" W (UTM 19/4988200mN 19/342200mE) on the USGS 15' quadrangle sheet titled "Second Connecticut Lake, New Hampshire/Maine (1927)."

The prehistoric site is normally covered by 1-3 meters of lake water. Since it lies within the boundary of a "Great Pond," it comes under the purview of the State of Maine. Land above the full basin mark of Aziscohos Lake (468 meters above sea level) is owned and managed by Boise Cascade Corporation. Tracts of timber, chiefly spruce and fir, are harvested periodically to supply pulp mills in Maine and New Hampshire. The immediate lakeshore is seldom molested by cutting operations and loggers take care to keep streams flowing into the lake free of pollutants. Beginning in 1960, four clusters of cottage lots on the east shore were leased and sold to sportsmen by the Brown Company of Berlin, New Hampshire. This partitioning was halted after a few score tracts were negotiated. No lots were sold in the immediate vicinity of the Adkins site, and the closest approach by road remains a rough track that ends at the mouth of Aldrich Brook a kilometer to the south of the archaeological site.

The right to control the level of Aziscohos Lake and the flow of the Magalloway River issuing from Aziscohos Dam belongs to the Union Water Power Company of Lewiston, Maine. A decision to reduce or increase lake level depends upon many factors, such as monthly precipitation, depth of snow-pack in the watershed, evaporation rate and industrial needs. For the sake of recreational boaters and fishermen, every effort is made to keep the lake as full as possible until Labor Day. Afterward, the lake may be drawn down as rapidly as 10 cm a day. Most years waters recede far enough to expose the Adkins site before fall rains replenish the lake. During droughts the site may be exposed long before Labor Day, and the barren lakebed is subject to erosion by wind, rain and runoff. As a rule, fall rains swell Aziscohos Lake sufficiently to inundate Adkins before freeze-up. Severe winter temperatures, for which northwestern highland Maine is notorious, promote the growth of thick ice on the lake. By spring the heavy ice cakes may be touching the lake bottom in shallow areas. The ice floats away during break-up, usually in April, but perhaps not before the blocks have plowed through sediments, displacing small boulders, and wreaking other havoc upon the shore. Considering the powerful erosive forces at work, it is a wonder that so much of the Adkins site escaped destruction. Any light-duty rock features such as boulder tent-rings and hearths surrounded by cobbles, of course, are likely to have been obliterated.

Aziscohos Dam was constructed at the head of a steep natural pitch with a fall of water of 75-80 m over one kilometer. These Falls of the Magalloway are unnavigable to any watercraft. During the nineteenth century residents of a nearby village, Wilsons Mills, hired out wagons and teams for portaging. Close to the river, on the right-hand bank proceeding upstream is a deeply worn path that winds among rocks and trees. This trail is likely an ancient carry or portage around the Falls — a legacy of generations of Indian hunters who traveled about interior Maine using lightweight birchbark canoes.

The present Aziscohos Dam was built in 1909-1911 on the site of a much smaller timber and earth dam that was erected in the late nineteenth century. The pool behind the dam was a great help to loggers and their operations. Logs harvested in the Magalloway watershed were floated to the lake during annual drives or hauled to water by teams of oxen and horses. Once ponded, rafts of logs were drawn down the lake to the dam by steam-powered towboats. Logs were chuted past the dam and into the Magalloway River bound for mills in Berlin, New Hampshire. The last long logs were driven to the mills in the 1930's (Rich 1942: 205), and the last drive of shorter pulp logs down the Magalloway and Androscoggin Rivers occurred in the early 1960's (Pinette 1986: 126). Since the 1950's, pulp logs began to be trucked to the mills.

Hundreds of miles of log-hauling roads were constructed throughout the Magalloway River catchment basin since 1950. These roads afforded easy access to regions that earlier could be reached only on foot or by boat. Before the existing Aziscohos Dam was erected, a trip to the Adkins site from the Falls of the Magalloway would have been slow by boat and arduous by land. Upstream of the Falls the river is deep and nearly free of rifts as far north as the forks of the Magalloway and Little Magalloway. Nevertheless, it is a meandering watercourse requiring twice the distance to be traveled by water than would be necessary by walking.

Halfway up Aziscohos Lake from the Dam, the Magalloway valley narrows and follows a S-course, forming in effect a natural baffle. The kink in the valley together with bedrock reefs crossing the valley floor at this point may have impeded the erosion of glacial outwash deposits, and large sections of an outwash plain and side-valley moraine were preserved. It is upon these ancient landforms, perched above the level of the modern river, that the Adkins encampment and other Palaeo-Indian sites are found.

The S-bend of the Magalloway valley is referred to as the Narrows. Steep rock ledge, in places rising sheer for 10-15 meters, hems in this part of the valley making entry or departure difficult. The Narrows would have been a logical place to intercept herd animals such as caribou moving up and down the Magalloway. Keeping to the valley floor, these animals would have had to thread their way among springs, kettle ponds and watercourses, offering good targets for Palaeo-Indian hunters.

The Adkins site is located at the narrowest section of the Narrows opposite a rocky ridge that projects, almost finger-like, from the western wall of the valley. Today the Magalloway River is far from the archaeological site, flowing near the western wall. Just where the river ran in Palaeo-Indian times is difficult to know as the pattern of its fossil meander scars (revealed by aerial photographs) is exceedingly complex. Some of these old meanders approach within 200-300 meters of the Adkins site, suggesting that the river shore may have been close at hand during the Palaeo-Indian occupation.

The prevailing wind direction, five out of six days, is from the northwest. The usual clear skies and cool temperatures are interrupted by flows of moisture-laden air from the west-southwest, culminating in violent storms and a return to strong winds from the northwest. This highly predictable monotonous weather pattern must have dictated the locations of Palaeo-Indian hunting camps. Camps would have been set up down-wind of kill sites. All confirmed Palaeo-Indian encampments are sited along the eastern margin of the valley where prevailing northwest winds would have wafted human scent away from approaching animal herds. Only during unsettled weather bringing rain or snow would the wind have betrayed the presence of hunters lying in ambush. The regular weather cycles of northwestern Maine must have been a boon to early hunters and may, in part, explain why they returned again and again to this region.

Bedrock in the vicinity of the Adkins site is fine-grained, badly cleaved meta-sediment of Palaeozoic age. It is unsuited for manufacturing flaked or ground stone tools. The sediment is interrupted in places by narrow felsite (likely rhyolite) dykes with chilled margins, but this raw material is soft and severely weathered. Tools made of it lack durable, sharp edges. The nearest occurrences of aphanitic rock with desirable fracturing properties are 25-30 km north of Adkins at Ledge Ridge and Thrasher Peaks. There can be found masses of multi-colored chert and coarser felsites of Cambro-Ordovician age (Wing and Dawson 1949). Gravels in the Magalloway valley contain felsite, greenstone and pebbles of tough, grainy red jasperoid derived from these rock bodies. There is, however, no high-grade chert to be seen in these gravels. Interesting to note, no tools or debitage of Ledge Ridge chert were unearthed at Adkins, and it appears that the site's ancient occupants were unaware of this lithic source.

Eighty kilometers south of Adkins is the Mt. Jasper lithic source — an outcropping of glassy, flow-banded rhyolite that was exploited from the Middle Archaic period onward (Gramly 1980, 1984b). Although this stone is well-suited for knapping, the outcrop is small and poorly exposed. It apparently went undetected by Palaeo-Indians.

Further afield, in central New Hampshire south of the White Mountains is a series of aphanitic volcanic, igneous and derived sedimentary rocks including the Moat Volcanics (Lalish 1979). Porphyritic felsites from this region were important to prehistoric groups. Felsites and related argillites, presumably Moat Volcanics, are well represented at the Adkins site but are only a minor element at Vail. They are absent altogether at other Palaeo-Indian sites in the upper Magalloway valley.

Also in the south, in central New Hampshire and adjacent Maine, are numerous pegmatites rich in massive quartz. Some of this quartz occurs in shapely crystals and is brilliantly clear, suited to optical needs. Quartz crystal was used sparingly, most often for scrapers (Nicholas 1981), in this part of New England during prehistory. It is found at the Adkins site and in small amounts at Upper Wheeler Dam, Lower Wheeler Dam and Vail. Artifacts of crystal quartz were also recovered in 1986 excavations at the Dam Palaeo-Indian site, near Wayne, Maine, by the Maine Historic Preservation Commission (Arthur Spiess, personal communication). However, fluted projectile points of crystal quartz, like those discovered from time to time in Virginia (McCary 1951), eastern Ontario (Roberts 1984), western Vermont (Loring 1980) and in the American West (Haury *et al.* 1959) are exceedingly scarce in north-central New England.

Apart from Ledge Ridge immediately north of Adkins, the nearest chert sources to the Magalloway valley lie in the Champlain Lowland of western Vermont and northeastern New York. Distances to outcrops range from 175 to 275 km. Another important lithic province is the Munsungan lithic source area of northern Piscataquis County, Maine, which lies approximately 225 km to the northeast of Aziscohos Lake (Bonnichsen *et al.* 1980, Bonnichsen 1985). None of the chert from Munsungan is present at Adkins, although it was used by the occupants of the Morss Palaeo-Indian site a few kilometers up the Magalloway valley.

Plant and animal resources are varied in the vicinity of the Adkins site today, in part, resulting from the man-made lake and environmental dislocations due to timber-cutting. Salmon, for example, were introduced to Aziscohos Lake for the benefit of sport fishermen; in pre-lake days there would have been only trout. Also, while loons nest on the lake today, it is doubtful if any of the small glacial ponds that once dotted the Magalloway valley would have been able to support such large birds for very long. Deer find forage in old wood-lots and along the open lake shore these days, but they may have been absent or much reduced in number when the region still had primeval forests.

Moose and forest caribou were the natural residents of the upper Magalloway valley, perhaps for the last several thousand years. Moose were nearly exterminated from this range 50 years ago, but carefully shepherded remnants of the Maine herd have successfully repopulated the region. Tracks of moose may be seen on any day along the shore of Aziscohos Lake. Caribou, however, suffered a sadder fate. Small local herds were shot off by 1900 and an attempt to reintroduce them to northern Maine (Wight 1985: 121) ended in failure. Caribou may have persisted in the headwaters region of the Magalloway River longer than in other parts of Maine due to the relative inaccessibility of this part of the state.

A curious feature of the upper Magalloway valley was a 10 km-long natural meadow, which extended north of the Vail site. Nineteenth century travellers (Stephens 1874) were impressed by the luxurient growth of bushes along this stretch of the valley. Willows, one of the favorite foods of caribou (Spiess 1979: 31; Palmer 1954: 305), were perhaps abundant in the meadow and were food for the Magalloway herds.

What game populated the Magalloway valley during the Palaeo-Indian era is conjectural. Between 11,000 and 10,000 years ago, locally tundra gave way to a mixed woodland and then to closed forest (Bombard and Davis 1985). For at least part of this millenium the upper Magalloway valley and surrounding hills would have been ideal caribou range with varying vegetation suited to the animals' seasonal needs. The well-watered future meadowland north of the Vail site may have been a favorite haunt of caribou even at this early date.

Although no bones or other food remains survived in the acidic forest soil of the Adkins site, it is reasonable to assume that caribou were the intended quarry of the Adkins hunters and the occupants of the other Magalloway valley Palaeo-Indian encampments. Caribou bone, present as calcined fragments, has been identified at two New England Palaeo-Indian sites (Spiess *et al.* 1984). One of these encampments, the Whipple fluted point site in southwestern New Hampshire, is strategically located for the interception of animal herds. It is reminiscent in every respect to the situation of the Adkins, Cox and Vail sites. Interesting to note, Vail and Whipple appear to be coeval (Curran 1984). Fluted points from Whipple and sites of the Magalloway valley are similar, affirming their close age.

Due to poor conditions of preservation, there is a bias towards viewing New England Palaeo-Indians as exclusive hunters of big game. Although their diet likely included divers plants and animals, such as fish that populated the Magalloway River, life in an Arctic-like environment would have been impossible without caribou. At some point during the year Palaeo-Indians would have to bag caribou or meet with other hunters to exchange goods for caribou products. In addition to meat, caribou furnish valuable hides, fat and antler. Among traditional Inuit, caribou hides were used primarily for clothing, tent-coverings, and sleeping bags or rugs for the home. The tundra and open woodlands of northern New England in this era may not have supported any other animal that could have substituted for the useful caribou.

The exposed location of the Adkins site, open to punishing, prevailing winds from the northwest, offered its inhabitants an uninterrupted view of several kilometers of the Magalloway valley. From this vantage point animals could be spotted in time for ambushes to be laid. The spot chosen by ancient hunters for their camp is very rocky with large, immovable boulders and bedrock close at hand. Sandier, more level tracts for an encampment lie nearby, but none of these spots may have been as well-drained as the slight, bouldery ridge where the Palaeo-Indian artifacts were unearthed.

Were it not for Aziscohos Lake, today the site would be covered with a mixed growth of birch, maple, oak, spruce, fir, larch and other species of a northern hardwood forest. In Palaeo-Indian times, it is doubtful if anything but tundra plants grew around the encampment. In sheltered nooks on the hillslopes behind the site, to be sure, there may have been dwarf spruce, shrubby birch and willow, which would have been useful for firewood.

The nearest stream to the Adkins site is Lincoln Brook, a few hundred meters to the south. To the north there are no other streams of consequence on the east side of the valley until the Morss site is reached. Springs abound, however, and the availability of water could hardly have been an important factor in dictating the location of this Palaeo-Indian station.

Apart from the Cox site, which lies a few hundred meters north of Adkins, the nearest archaeological occurrences are scattered flaked stone artifacts along Aldrich and Lincoln Brooks close to their confluences with the Magalloway River. None of the 48 artifacts reported from these places can be assigned confidently to a specific archaeological culture or time period. Further, many artifacts are fashioned of grainy raw materials with poor fracturing properties (Gramly 1985b: 118, 119), which were rarely employed by Palaeo-Indian knappers except as hammerstones, hammer-anvils and other heavy-duty implements. On the face of it, these finds appear to mark Neo-Indian occupations along the brooks, perhaps dating to the Archaic period. Occupation was brief as so few objects were discarded. Important to note, ground stone tools are absent. In northwestern Maine ground stone tools are found commonly only at Archaic sites in extremely favorable locations for fisheries, e.g., at the outlet of a lake. Repeated occupations for lengthy periods would be expected at such special spots.

Another presumed Neo-Indian site within a short distance of Adkins is Metallac's Pond (Gramly *ibid.*). It is located roughly a kilometer southwest of the Vail encampment along the margin of the elevated glacial outwash plain occupied by Vail, Wight and the Vail kill sites #1 and #2. The badly weathered condition of the felsite tools and debitage discovered there suggest considerable antiquity; yet, typical Palaeo-Indian artifacts are absent. This fact and the observation that Middle and Late Archaic groups made heavy use of felsite for their flaked implements lead one to believe that Metallac's Pond is an Archaic encampment. The abundance of flake knives and dearth of projectile points indicate that it may have been used only a few times as a fishing camp.

Farther up the Magalloway valley are additional Neo-Indian sites, which are located for the most part close to the modern river channel wherever there are sandy knolls and terraces. Neo-Indian camps may be expected at confluences of small streams and the Magalloway River. Some sites evidence reoccupation over thousands of years, to judge by variation in styles of projectile points and raw materials used in their manufacture. Most Archaic flaked tools are fashioned of fine-grained igneous rocks and white (milky) quartz. Chert appears to have been preferred during the Palaeo-Indian era as well as the Ceramic Period (500 B.C. - A.D. 1600). This curious predilection for specific raw materials by archaeological cultures of northern New England is well known (Gramly 1980, 1984b), and it has broader regional implications as well (Meltzer 1984, Hoffman 1985).

None of the known Magalloway valley Neo-Indian sites appears to be as large or as productive as Vail. Without excavating it is difficult to estimate accurately the extent and volume of debris present at these encampments. The scattered artifacts and fire-cracked rock features exposed by lake erosion are not very impressive, and most Neo-Indian camps seem to be small. During any episode of occupation the amount of lithic debris that was added to a site likely did not exceed, or perhaps even equal, the amount deposited at the Adkins site.

We may infer that throughout the 9,500 years assigned to the Archaic and Ceramic Periods the upper Magalloway valley was lightly trafficked. Occupations were either brief or occurred infrequently. By comparison during the Palaeo-Indian era, the valley was utilized intensively, likely in the same season year after year. This idea is supported by the homogeneous style of fluted point that is common to all the Magalloway encampments. Debris at all stations accumulated within the "lifetime" of a single style of projectile point, viz., the moderately to deeply concave, straight-sided fluted point characteristic of the Debert site, Nova Scotia. The longevity of this artifact type is likely reckoned in terms of generations but certainly not in thousands of years.

If caribou were the objective of the Magalloway Palaeo-Indian band, then 20-30 year periods of exploitation would have alternated with intervals during which the valley was abandoned. Caribou, like many other wild animals, suffer declines or are forced by hunger to abandon preferred grounds (Burch 1971). Hunters who depended upon them for clothing and food would have behaved similarly.

The Magalloway Valley Palaeo-Indian Complex

Palaeo-Indian sites of the upper Magalloway valley appear to belong to a brief period of New England culture prehistory, likely a single phase, as evidenced by the similarity of projectile points from all components (see **Plate 13**).

Fluted points from Adkins, Morss, the Wheeler Dam sites and Vail (including kill sites #1 and #2) are moderately to deeply concave with a depth of basal concavity ranging from five to sixteen mm. All points from these sites were once straight-sided or gently flaring outward from the base. Normally there is only one channel flake per face, which extends at most half-way along the length of the point. All completed points, except heavily resharpened and reworked specimens, exhibit edge grinding along the lower margin of the cutting edges and usually within the basal concavity. Points are moderately thick (6-10 mm) and relatively wide, in most cases exceeding 24 mm in width. The author has argued that fluted points of these dimensions tipped thrusting spears, not javelins (Gramly 1984a).

Fluted points from the Magalloway sites are similar to, and perhaps are developed from, projectile points of the Bull Brook Phase (Grimes *et al.* 1984: 172). They closely resemble fluted points from the Debert site (MacDonald 1968), but they are more deeply concave than points illustrated from other well-known Palaeo-Indian sites in the Northeast, such as Shoop (Witthoft 1952) and West Athens Hill (Ritchie and Funk 1973). In the central Great Lakes region, which includes Ontario, deeply concave, straight-sided fluted points are termed "Gainey points" (Deller and Ellis n.d.) after an extensive encampment in Michigan of that name where many specimens were unearthed

(Simons *et al.* 1984).

Besides deeply concave, straight-sided fluted points, the stations of the Magalloway Valley Palaeo-Indian Complex share other flaked tool types, as follows: sidescrapers; trianguloid endscrapers; narrow, slug-shaped unifaces known as *limaces,* flake-shavers or groovers; a variety of cutters including flaked gravers and utilized flakes; and *pièces esquillées.* In many cases this latter tool type was recycled from an exhausted trianguloid endscraper.

Fluted drills, bifacially flaked knives or projectile point preforms, snapped gravers (a form of cutter), burins, hammerstones, anvils, and stone awls belong on the trait-list of the complex; however, these forms are relatively rare and may not occur at small sites with but a single episode of occupation — like Adkins.

Common to all members of the site complex is a preference by ancient knappers for fine-grained or glassy raw materials. Stones that are superlative for flaking are unevenly distributed about New England, and the extent of outcrops at a given source may be limited, as for example, Ledge Ridge in the Magalloway valley. The acumen shown by Palaeo-Indians in locating some lithic sources is cause for marvel. Obviously, hunters paid close attention to stream gravels and outcrop wherever they wandered. Chance finds of crystal pockets or fine-grained glacial erratics may have dictated that a hunter sit down and produce some tools, or at least reduce raw material to easily transportable form, before continuing a journey.

Another trait of the Magalloway Valley Palaeo-Indian Complex is the construction of caches. Two caches, one at Vail (Feature 2) and the other at Adkins, have been recognized. Others may have existed but were mis-identified as natural hollows with washed-in artifacts (*cf.* Gramly 1982: 21 and Map 7). In-ground caches might be located several meters away from remains of Palaeo-Indian habitations and could be overlooked by excavators intent upon recovering flaked stone artifacts. The cache at the Adkins encampment with its ring of massive boulders could hardly pass unnoticed; but at other sites in the Magalloway valley boulders are in short supply and timber and earth may have been used for construction instead of rock.

All sites belonging to the Magalloway Valley Palaeo-Indian Complex have been entered upon the register of the Maine Historic Preservation Commission, Augusta, Maine. Every confirmed Palaeo-Indian encampment (Vail, Adkins, Morss, Wheeler Dam sites, Cox and Wight) has been explored. Other sites, particularly, small ones like Adkins and Cox, may have been obliterated by the grinding ice and waves of Aziscohos Lake. During clement weather at rare times of low lake level searches for additional Palaeo-Indian stations continue. The success of this enterprise to date suggests that the upper Magalloway valley was a favorite haunt of Palaeo-Indian hunters, to which they returned perhaps for generations.

Method of Excavation and Discoveries

The Adkins site was found on September 16, 1984, by Warden Charles Adkins of Rangeley, Maine, and Alexandra Morss, working under the supervision of the writer. Adkins and Morss were scanning the rocky shore of a shallow cove at the Narrows of Aziscohos Lake **(Plates 3, 5 and 6)** when the first flaked tools were observed lying on a bank of sand and gravel **(Plate 7)**. This section of the Magalloway valley had not yielded artifacts during reconnoitering in 1979-1983, and the discovery was a welcome surprise.

A base-line was established immediately and 20 tools and flakes exposed upon the surface were plotted in relation to it and afterwards collected. No excavation was attempted that day and further visiting was deferred until a proper investigation could be mounted.

Late in September a field party directed by the writer, which included volunteer excavators from the Maine Historic Preservation Commission, returned to Adkins. Our expectations were not high that any of the archaeological deposit had escaped erosion; therefore, rather large grid-squares (2 m) were adopted as the units of excavation. The season being late and the onset of bitter weather expected at any time, a relatively coarse mesh (6 mm) was employed for sieving. Excavations were hurried along for fear that collectors or inquisitive sportsmen would molest the site and remove artifacts during our absence.

In retrospect, none of our concerns and fears were well grounded. Collectors were cooperative and, recognizing the importance of the discovery, they did not disturb the excavation. Also, it proved to be one of the warmest fall seasons on record for northern New England, and day after day skies remained cloudless. Most important for our research, however, was the fact that many artifacts remained *in situ.* Miraculously, humus and the underlying forest soil zones had survived in places, including the sector with the densest concentration of stone tools and waste.

Having excavated six 2-m grid-squares, much of the remaining area was investigated in more manageable 1-m grids. In each unit a distinction was made between an erosional lag sand and the underlying, undisturbed forest soil. Artifacts in both the lag sand and forest soil were plotted piece by piece in relation to the site's master grid **(Figures 7 and 8)**. Of course, many small objects, chiefly tool fragments and fine debitage, were overlooked during troweling. To a great degree these specimens were captured on the sieves and were tallied for each grid-square **(Figure 9)**.

A map showing the appearance of the forest soil (and thus the degree of erosion) was made for each grid after the lag sand had been cleared away. Taken together, these maps **(Figure 6)** provide an overview of the extent of erosion of Adkins.

A close watch was maintained for hearths, pits and postholes. Many excavators were veterans of the 1980-82 fieldwork at Vail and had learned what sorts of features might be expected. Apart from the stone structure itself, no Palaeo-Indian features were encountered within the excavated area.

Lag sand and forest soil were passed through a 6 mm (¼ inch) mesh. Dry sieving was used in most of our work although the contents of two 2-m squares were processed in water. While it was easy to spot fine flakes and tool fragments by sieving in water, any artifacts passing through the mesh were lost. The spoil pile accumulated by dry sieving was allowed to stand until May, 1985, and then reworked. A 3 mm (1/8 inch) mesh in water was employed. This operation netted 112 tiny flakes, flake fragments, tool fragments and a few large specimens that were accidentally overlooked during the first round of sieving with a coarser mesh.

The positions of 144 flaked stone artifacts were plotted on the grid for the Adkins site; 78 of these objects lay in the lag sand, and the remainder were within the primary context of forest soil. Using a 6 mm mesh sieve, 178 artifacts were garnered. The majority (130) were derived from lag sand. The above counts, when added to the tally obtained by reworking the spoil earth pile and the tally of objects whose findspots are unknown, total 438.

Undobutedly many very small specimens were passed over, especially during wet-sieving. The combined weights of these missing specimens must be slight, perhaps only one or two percent of the weight of the full assemblage. By most standards, artifact recovery at Adkins was good for labor out-of-doors often under trying conditions.

After only a few days of excavations it became apparent that artifacts were clustered. The principal cluster was oval and measured 2.5 m by 3 m. It and a small lobe or extension running to the west contained 116 specimens whose locations were known well enough to be plotted as points (**Figure 10**). One and one-half meters west of the main cluster lay 14 additional artifacts. This small group was linked to the main mass by conjoined fragments of a sidescraper (A-43 and A-102) and a flake group (A-21, A-28, A-98 and A-291).

Apart from the two clusters, artifacts were scarce. Interestingly, 11 of the 12 plotted specimens that were unearthed away from the concentrations circumscribe an area approximately five meters in diameter. It is difficult to explain this distribution as a fortuitous product of erosion by Aziscohos Lake. Four of the artifacts in the arc were *in situ* within forest soil; the remainder lay in lag sand resting upon truncated forest soil.

Most of the stone tools and debitage at the Adkins encampment, like the Vail site, occurred at the contact between the forest humus and the underlying A_2-zone. Undoubtedly they had lain near the surface of the ground for 10,000-11,000 years; during part of this period arctic and sub-arctic conditions prevailed in the Magalloway valley. Some pieces may have been displaced from their original resting places by frost, animals and other non-cultural agencies. An experimental study in Alaska has shown that neat patterns of stone flakes become disorganized after only a few years of exposure in an arctic environment (Bowers *et al.* 1983). Over long periods tight clusters of flaking debris would be diffused and expanded in size. This prediction, which was generated by computers using observed parameters, suggests that the Adkins clusters may have been even more sharply defined at the time they were laid down than now.

While it is certain that the general distribution of flaked tools and waste at Adkins is a product of Palaeo-Indian behavior, what these actions may have been is conjectural. The arc of artifacts and both clusters are tied together by conjoined tool fragments — an indication that all three units were deposited at about the same time. In the writer's opinion the principal cluster of debris represents a heavily trafficked work area just inside the door of a dwelling, while the lobate extension of the oval cluster may mark the sitting place of workers just outside and to one side of the entry. At these places Palaeo-Indians may have sat, resharpened tools and performed sundry domestic tasks. The arc of artifacts may be viewed as the outline of a tent or lodge, perhaps the back wall. From time to time objects may have been discarded or swept up against this wall, likely where it met the ground. If this idea were correct, then the lune-shaped bare area between the interior work station and tent wall must have been reserved for sleeping.

The small cluster of artifacts west of the presumed tent entrance may represent a dump for household sweepings or offal. It lay within easy pitching distance of a person standing in the doorway.

No trace of a hearth was noted within the confines of the Adkins dwelling or anywhere else at the site. If fire were used at all (and one might expect the work area of the tent to have been illuminated at night) it may have been confined to a firebox or lamp. While awaiting the caribou herds to arrive in the valley and during the period of the hunt, the Adkins group may have eschewed fire and cooking for fear that the scent would alarm their quarry. Even at the Vail site, which was repeatedly occupied over many years, there was scant physical evidence of hearths, cooking and fire. Only Feature 1, a 30 cm-deep pit containing abundant charcoal and artifacts (many showing the effects of heating), could be termed a hearth without any reservation.

While the main excavation was underway at Adkins, a close pattern of shovel test-holes was made around the site in search of other habitations. The bare sand and gravel also were searched meticulously for flakes and tools. Nothing at all was discovered.

Adkins and Upper Wheeler Dam are the only Palaeo-Indian encampments in the Magalloway valley with single habitations and no signs of reoccupation. In the case of Vail, and likely Morss and Lower Wheeler Dam as well, it has been demonstrated (Gramly 1982) that upon any occasion at least two habitations may have stood at the site. Reoccupation of the Vail encampment, perhaps in successive years, seems likely. The Cox site stands apart from the above Palaeo-Indian stations due to the small number of artifacts recovered there and the restricted nature of its assemblage. It may have been a briefly occupied hunters' camp.

Single-dwelling Palaeo-Indian sites like Adkins and Upper Wheeler Dam are known for other regions as well. For example, at the Paleo-II-W site located along the Holcombe Beach, Macomb County, Michigan (Fitting *et al.* 1966), artifacts were confined to an area of 35 feet in diameter. Prior to cultivation this locus may have been even smaller and more focused. Like Adkins, Paleo-II-W yielded no hearths, but keen-eyed excavators did note two faint postholes within the cluster of artifacts. Interestingly, the postholes were 13 feet apart, and a dwelling comparable in size to the Adkins structure is suggested.

The scarcity of postholes on Palaeo-Indian encampments in glaciated North America cannot be ascribed to sloppy fieldwork by inattentive archaeologists. Even if the fill of all postholes were thoroughly leached and blended with the colors of surrounding soils, one would expect to find artifacts where posts were set. Not one feature even remotely resembling a posthole was encountered at Vail although it is surmised that two families or hunting parties camped there as many as 30 times (Gramly 1985a). At the 6LF21 site in northwestern Connecticut (also known as the Templeton site) only one posthole was observed in the Palaeo-Indian zone, and no trace of a pattern of postholes was reported (Moeller 1980, 1984). The dearth of structural remains at Vail, 6LF21 and scores of other Palaeo-Indian stations implies that the occupants used tents with few supporting posts anchored in earth.

A notable aspect of the Adkins site is the large number of boulders there; during the Palaeo-Indian occupation when tundra likely existed, most of these boulders would have been visible. Their surfaces would have provided good workplaces and seats. Some of the rocks may have been rearranged as a matter of convenience. Arctic dwellers, such as the Greenland Inuit, incorporated natural rock features into their constructions (Thostrup 1917), and light, portable boulders were used to weight down the skirts of tents **(Plate 14)**. The Adkins Palaeo-Indians may have done the same, but the grinding ice of Aziscohos Lake would have obliterated all arrangements except the most cyclopean constructions.

At the onset of the September excavations at Adkins, a curious oval grouping of heavy boulders was observed immediately adjacent to the artifact clusters. At its widest, the oval measured three meters. After working several days and completing a contour map of the site's surface and its many rocks, we grew convinced that the oval was artificial. The feature appeared to be filled and surrounded with lag sand **(Plate 9)**, and as a first step, sand inside was removed.

The lag sand masked a shallow (22 cm deep), egg-shaped pit with sloping sides that had been dug into hard, greenish-tan glacial outwash. The lower 10-15 cm of the pit was filled with layered sand, gray in color, which gave off a musty smell of mouldered vegetation or bog. Apparently the pit had been open to the sky for a long period and had held water and decayed plants.

Four of the large rocks rimming the pit jutted inward, in effect, partially roofing it **(Figure 11)**. The other large boulders seemed to have been stationary at the time the hole was made by Palaeo-Indians. They may have served as anchors for the entire construction.

Gaps between the heavy rocks were sealed with smaller boulders. Most scavengers, such as foxes, would have been unable to penetrate this barrier. On the north side of the structure was a 40 cm-wide opening facing north. This gap among the rocks may have been a door, and a large rounded boulder that lay nearby would have served admirably as a doorstone.

No artifacts or food remains were discovered inside the structure or immediately around it. Three small boulders were noted at the doorway in the pit bottom. These rocks may have slumped down the side of the pit; but not recently, as they lay embedded in the gray, layered sand and were well below the lag sand deposited by Aziscohos Lake.

The absence of domestic debris and the structure's small size rule against the idea that it was a domicile. Inuit houses of piled rocks were much roomier than the Adkins structure, with diameters of 3-4 meters or greater (Boas 1884). Small-sized, circular shelters measuring 2-3 meters in diameter were employed by Inuit hunters (Hawkes 1916). The walls of hunters' shelters stood 1-2 meters high, quite unlike the Adkins feature with its walls that appear to have never been more than a course high. Another argument against the notion the Adkins stone chamber was a house or shelter is the low ceiling height. The interior space is awkward and cramped for an adult human being.

People of the Arctic who employ stone as building material have a rich repertoire of constructions including: "house walls, store chambers, tent-rings, frameworks for [supporting] kayaks and umiaks, and meat cellars" (Rasmussen 1927: 44). Burial chambers were also made of butted stones.

The permanent meat storage chambers or cellars of the Inuit closely resemble the Adkins stone feature. They and the Adkins feature are quite unlike Inuit temporary meat stores, which are expedient constructions made by heaping boulders of a size that any man could lift. Temporary stores lack the interlocked, carefully positioned rocks of the Adkins feature. Inuit permanent meat stores, however, are composed of accurately fitted stones of great size (Thostrup 1917: 200-201), and according to Freuchen and Salomonsen these caches must be extremely strong as bears are able to move the largest stones that a man can lift (1958: 51). Also, in the opinion of Jenness, wolverines are able to dislodge any stone that two men working together could lift and carry (1928: 65).

The Adkins structure is built primarily of rocks weighing 100 kg or more. Such massive stones must have been pushed or dragged into place; they could not have been lifted by two men, or even four, and moved any great distance without mishap. With a roof of logs and rocks covered by earth and frozen hard by saturating it with water, the Adkins permanent meat store would have kept out most animals. Even foxes, which are reputed to be able to worm their way into the smallest crevices (Jenness 1928: 106), would have been stymied by the packed stones.

If one believes that a flat roof of logs or other materials covered the Adkins stone structure, then the volume of the chamber thus formed would have been .56 cubic meter. A cavity of this size, which is nearly three times the capacity of most household refrigerators, could accommodate the deboned flesh of 11-14 caribou, depending upon the sex of the butchered animals. This statistic is based upon Spiess' observations that a 110 kg caribou bull yields approximately 50 kg of edible flesh and that a female caribou weighing 80 kg has 40 kg of usable flesh (1979: 28-29). The computation assumes that a liter of flesh weighs roughly a kilogram.

Considering that a family of four Caribou Eskimo may require as many as 200 caribou to nourish itself through the year and perhaps an additional 50 animals for their dogs (Burch 1972: 362), then a cache of only 11-14 animals would hardly have provisioned a party of Palaeo-Indians subsisting upon a meat diet for very long. Such a small food depot might have been utilized by a hunting party who remained in the Magalloway valley after the main kill had been made in order to explore their new surroundings. Also, a supply of stored meat would have been welcome to a hunting party returning the next year to set up an ambush in the valley for caribou. Under arctic or near-arctic conditions meat in semi-subterranean cellar keeps well — its toothsomeness enhanced by long aging.

After investigation of the stone structure was completed, it was filled with large gravel in order to protect it from the rising waters of Aziscohos Lake. Before it was inundated, however, a decision was made to dismantle the structure and to transport it to the Maine State Museum in Augusta, Maine, for use in an exhibit. Since access to the Adkins site was nearly impossible by vehicle, even when equipped with large tires and chains, the assistance of a National Guard helicopter and cargo net for hauling away stones were required. Under the supervision of Dr. Bruce Bourque of the Maine State Museum, the cache was taken apart. Each rock was numbered, and numerous photographs were made of the operation. This work was carried out in early November, and none too soon, for frost had begun to penetrate the ground (**Plates 10 and 11**).

As already noted, excavations at Adkins continued in May of the following year (1985) when the spoil pile that had accumulated beside the trenches was resieved with a fine mesh. Permanent grid markers of metal rod were established at points N0E0 and N0E46 — the latter point well above the reach of lake waters and ice.

Raw Materials and the Assemblage

No Neo-Indian remains were discovered at the Adkins site. It may be assumed that the entire flaked stone assemblage, including debitage, resulted from tool maintenance and production by Palaeo-Indians.

The 1984-87 archaeological excavation encompassed the portion of the site with artifacts. No deposits that were suspected of containing artifacts were left undug. The yield was 438 specimens — a total that was reduced to 417 objects after fragments had been joined. This tally was attained by at first sieving excavated earth with a 6 mm (¼-inch) mesh and then later with a 3 mm (1/8-inch) mesh. A few square meters of the site with the densest concentration of artifacts were processed in water with the coarser mesh only. It is likely that some flakes, tool fragments and perhaps a few very small, whole tools escaped through the sieve and were lost. The weight of these unrecovered specimens is reckoned to be only a few grams. The weight of the entire assemblage was nearly a kilogram (Table 1).

It is remarkable that no fewer than 14 varieties of raw material are represented in the assemblage. This fact is in harmony with the peripatetic lifestyle of Palaeo-Indians who dwelled in formerly glaciated northeastern North America. Elsewhere, Palaeo-Indian assemblages feature fewer stone varieties, and the bulk of raw materials was obtained from outcrops and gravels lying close at hand (Meltzer and Smith 1986: 15). The heterogeneity of the Adkins assemblage also may indicate that the knappers relied upon no single source of raw material. At this particular period the Adkins group may have had no established patterns of movement that brought them back to the same lithic sources year after year.

Of the 417 flaked stone specimens at Adkins, 141 or 34% are tools and tool fragments. The ratio of tool and tool fragments to debitage is approximately 1:2.

By way of comparison, Locus H, the only habitation locus at the Vail site to have escaped erosion and collecting by relic-seekers, yielded 282 tools and flakes. Tools and tool fragments (tallied after matching fragments had been restored) at Locus H amounted to 36% of the assemblage, and the ratio of tools and tool fragments to debitage approached 1:2. Like Adkins, Locus H had been occupied only once by Palaeo-Indians. Artifacts at Locus H were, on the whole, smaller and more fragmentary than those at Adkins. This observation implies that either the Adkins band arrived in the Magalloway valley better supplied with lithics or the stones used by them were tougher and not as liable to fracture during use.

Shaped tools (scrapers, awls, coronet flaked gravers, *limaces,* fluted points and drills, bifaces, burins, *etc.*) are rare at Adkins and Vail Locus H, amounting to only 9% and 8% respectively of their total inventories of artifacts. At both sites there are approximately twice as many unshaped tools (*e.g., pièces esquillées,* utilized flakes, *etc.*) as there are shaped tools.

A low proportion of shaped or "formal" tools, that is, tools that show extensive retouching or bifacial flaking, is characteristic of sites belonging to the Magalloway Valley Palaeo-Indian Complex. The most abundant tools in all assemblages of the Complex are cutters, particularly expedient varieties such as utilized flakes and becs. Together with *pièces esquillées,* cutters far outnumber trianguloid endscrapers, bifaces and other shaped implements (*cf.* Gramly 1982: 22).

The preponderance of informal or unshaped tools, as seen at northwestern Maine encampments, is not universal among Palaeo-Indian assemblages of northeastern North America. At the Holcombe site, for example, the sample of 385 tools included an impressive quantity (110) of projectile points and fragments (Fitting 1975: 47). Various stations of the Parkhill Complex also appear to have relatively small numbers of informal, unshaped tools (*cf.* Ellis 1984: Table 87 for a summary).

TABLE 1.
Tallies and Weights of Raw Material Varieties of Flaked Tools and Debitage, Adkins Site.

Raw Material Variety	Number of Objects*	Weight (grams)
1. Dark gray, finely banded felsite, weathers light olive-gray	115	765.8
2. Grayish-black porphyritic felsite, weathers yellowish-gray	39	229.7
3. Crystal quartz	140	184.6
4. Grayish-red to dusky-red chert or silicified argillite	17	44.0
5. Mottled dark gray and olive-gray chert	16	36.5
6. Dark gray to dark yellowish-brown lineated aphanitic stone	1	33.4
7. Grayish-black chert with many vesicles	4	29.8
8. White (milky) quartz	47	26.3
9. Grayish-black chert with quartz speherules	11	25.6
10. Grayish-black chert, mottled, badly jointed with many vesicles	7	7.2
11. Grayish-red chert	2	5.0
12. Fine olive-gray quartzite	6	.7
13. Lustrous dark reddish-brown chert	1	.1
14. Greenstone: greenish-gray groundmass with black spherules	8**	595.6
15. Unidentified raw materials	3	2.5
TOTALS	**417**	**1986.8**

*Whole objects only; fitted fragments counted as one.
**Includes a hammerstone weighing 510 grams.

This variability in the gross composition of Palaeo-Indian tool assemblages is not easily explained. The large number of utilized flakes present at a lithic workshop such as the West Athens Hill site in eastern New York state (Ritchie and Funk 1973: 27) might be expected since a person needing a tool had a tremendous selection of raw material in all shapes and sizes and there was no need for economy. At the Vail site by contrast, a large number of informal tools resulted from knappers recycling worn-out formal tools — a good example of this process being the conversion of a trianguloid endscraper to a *pièce esquillée*. The need for so many informal tools at Adkins and Vail (Locus H) may have resulted from the processing of whole caribou there. Other explanations might have to be marshalled to explain the observed ratios between informal and formal tools at other Palaeo-Indian sites. The real explanation for the particular character of the Magalloway Valley assemblages may be unknowable given the disappearance of all ancient organics (wood, bone) after millenia of weathering. Whatever the underlying cause, the ratio is remarkably consistent among all encampments of the Magalloway Valley Palaeo-Indian Complex.

In analyzing a stone tool assemblage it is instructive to ascertain what tools were resharpened or recycled on site. By sorting flaking debris into separate raw materials according to flake varieties, the presence of specific tools may be surmised. It is not unusual to discover that tools were resharpened or recycled at an encampment but later carried off to another place. Such behavior may have occurred at the Potts Palaeo-Indian site in Oswego County, New York, where many uniface resharpening flakes of exotic stone were unearthed but few matching tools (Gramly and Lothrop 1984: 134). Of the six varieties of colorful, exotic chert represented at the site, only one remained at the encampment in the form of an exhausted uniface. Similarly, at Adkins a biface of white quartz was reduced (**Table 11**), perhaps to a fluted projectile point, but the end-product was not recovered in our excavations. Other examples of "missing" tools are given in **Table 2**.

TABLE 2.
Tools That Were Reduced, Resharpened or Recycled at the Adkins Site (Minimum = 20; maximum = 58).

Tool	Raw Material	Identity
1. Biface	Fine olive-gray quartzite	Not found
2. Biface	Grayish-red to dusky-red chert or silicified argillite	Not found
3. Biface	Grayish-black chert, mottled, badly jointed with many vesicles	Not found
4. Biface	White (milky) quartz	Not found
5. Biface	Dark gray, finely banded felsite, weathers light olive-gray	Conjoined fluted point preform (A-1/A-2)
6. Biface	Grayish-black prophyritic felsite, weathers yellowish-gray	Not found
7. Hammerstone	Greenstone	Not found (Note: the flakes of this raw material appear to be derived from a hammerstone other than A-91)
8. *Pièce esquillée*	Crystal quartz	Any or all: A-14; A-81; A-180; A-201; A-202; A-241; A-246; A-259; A-269; A-279; A-315; A-362; A-411; A-425; A-430; A-439; A-446
9. *Pièce esquillée*	Dark gray, finely banded felsite, weathers light olive-gray	Conjoined specimens — A-19/A-51/A-90/A-121/A-173
10. *Pièce esquillée*	Grayish-black porphyritic felsite, weathers yellowish-gray	Fragment of a sidescraper used as a *pièce esquillée* (A-288)
11. Sidescraper	Grayish-black porphyritic felsite, weathers yellowish-gray	Fragment of a larger, broken side-scraper, which was reused (A-43)
12. Uniface	Grayish-black chert with quartz spherules	Any or all: A-61; A-426; A-431 (endscrapers)
13. Uniface	Grayish-red chert	Not found
14. Uniface	Lustrous dark reddish-brown chert	Not found
15. Uniface	Grayish-red to dusky-red chert or silicified argillite	Derived from sidescraper (A-4)
16. Uniface	Grayish-black chert, mottled, badly jointed with many vesicles	Perhaps cutters, variety flaked graver (A-60 and A-110)
17. Uniface	Mottled dark gray and olive-gray chert	Not found
18. Uniface	Crystal quartz	Any or all: A-9; A-24; A-154; A-223; A-248; A-271; A-274; A-277; A-282; A-319; A-423; A-424; A-429 (end-scrapers and sidescrapers)
19. Uniface	Dark gray, finely banded felsite, weathers light olive-gray	Sidescrapers (A-5/A-27; A-35; A-30; A-442; A-443), trianguloid end-scraper (A-92), *limaces*/groovers (A-6; A-10) — any or all
20. Uniface	Grayish-black porphyritic felsite, weathers yellowish-gray	*Limace*/groover (A-18)

Tools that were resharpened or recycled on site were likely used there or somewhere nearby, as in the case of the kill sites west of the Vail encampment. The recovery of tools but no associated debitage poses a problem for a stone tool analyst. It cannot be proved that these implements were put into service while the site was occupied. Heavily worn implements that were discarded on site might have been culled from tool-kits of departing hunters who were reducing the weight of their baggage. In some cases still useful tools might be cached to be retrieved at another time. It has been argued that at the Vail site there was at least one instance when a servicable tool was secreted — a large sidescraper in Feature 2 (Gramly 1982: 59). Although no caches of stone tools were recognized at Adkins, it is notable that many large, undamaged cutters were unearthed within the principal artifact cluster. Perhaps they and other tools no longer present (?) were deposited to be reclaimed as future need and shortages of lithic raw material dictated.

At least 126 stone tools were discarded at Adkins **(Table 3)**; however, an inspection of debitage and conjoined artifacts suggests that a maximum of only 58 tools was used at the site **(Table 2).** Cutters figure heavily among abandoned tools, but none of the small flakes that would have broken off their edges during use were recovered in our excavation. Conversely, at least six bifaces were reduced or resharpened at the encampment, but only three bifaces (fluted point preform, two fluted points) came to rest there. The apparent under-representation of cutters and bifaces in these different tablulations demonstrates the need for caution by any analyst who hopes to infer what the working tool-kit of a Palaeo-Indian hunting band may have been. The standard equation that tool presence in an archaeological deposit equals tool use has limiting conditions and must be applied with caution.

Although it is not possible to quantify it in any meaningful way, the tool-kit that the Adkins Palaeo-Indians brought with them to the Magalloway valley was rich in bifaces and large sharp flakes. These large flakes could have been adapted to several uses, as the occasion demanded. With unifacial retouching they became sidescrapers; broken into fragments and retouched, they yielded various scrapers and cutters. More often, one suspects, they were left unmodified and were used as simple cutting in-

TABLE 3.
Tools That Were Discarded at the Adkins Site
(Includes Uniface and Cutter Fragments).

Tool	Raw Material	Identity
1. Biface	Dark gray, finely banded felsite, weathers light olive-gray	A-1/A-2 plus conjoined flake
2. Fluted point	Dark gray, finely banded felsite, weathers light olive-gray	A-7
3. Fluted point	Grayish-black porphyritic felsite, weathers yellowish-gray	A-3
4. Hammerstone	Greenstone	A-91
5. *Pièce esquillée*	Crystal quartz	A-14; A-81; A-180; A-201; A-202; A-241; A-246; A-259; A-269; A-279; A-315; A-362; A-411; A-425; A-430; A-439; A-446
6. *Pièce esquillée*	Mottled dark gray and olive-gray chert	A-58
7. *Pièce esquillée*	Grayish-black porphyritic felsite, weathers yellowish-gray	A-288

8. *Pièce esquillée*	Dark gray, finely banded felsite; weathers light olive gray	Conjoined pieces A-19/A-51/A-90/A-121/ A-173
9. Sidescraper	Grayish-red to dusky-red chert or silicified argillite	A-4
10. Sidescraper	Dark gray to dark yellowish-brown lineated aphanitic stone	A-25
11. Sidescraper	Crystal quartz	A-24
12. Sidescraper	Dark gray, finely banded felsite, weathers light olive-gray	Conjoined pieces A-5/A-27/A-374; A-30; A-47; A-442; A-443
13. Sidescraper	Grayish-black porphyritic felsite, weathers yellowish-gray	A-43
14. Sidescraper	Mottled dark gray and olive-gray chert	A-31/A-115
15. Uniface	Grayish-black chert with many vesicles	A-36; A-441
16. Uniface	Dark gray, finely banded felsite, weathers light olive-gray	A-415
17. Trianguloid endscraper	Grayish-black chert with quartz spherules	A-61; A-426; A-431
18. Trianguloid endscraper	Grayish-black chert with many vesicles	A-427; A-428
19. Trianguloid endscraper	Crystal quartz	A-9; A-154; A-223; A-248; A-271; A-274 A-277; A-282; A-319; A-423; A-424; A-429
20. Trianguloid endscraper	Dark gray, finely banded felsite, weathers light olive-gray	A-92
21. *Limace*/groover	Grayish-black porphyritic felsite, weathers yellowish-gray	A-18
22. *Limace*/groover	Dark gray, finely banded felsite, weathers light olive-gray	A-6; A-10
23. Cutter (variety utilized flake)	Grayish-black chert with quartz spherules	A-100
24. Cutter ″	Grayish-red chert	A-186
25. Cutter ″	Grayish-black chert with many vesicles	A-42
26. Cutter ″	Grayish-black chert, mottled, badly jointed with many vesicles	A-106; A-118
27. Cutter ″	Mottled dark gray and olive-gray chert	A-37/A-95; A-44
28. Cutter ″	Crystal quartz	A-3; A-13; A-64; A-83; A-150; A-151; A-172; A-243; A-245; A-256; A-262 A-270; A-273; A-304; A-306; A-311; A-333; A-338; A-346; A-410
29. Cutter ″	Dark gray, finely banded felsite, weathers light olive-gray	A-12; A-15; A-16; A-20; A-22; A-35; A-34/A-49; A-45; A-59; A-136; A-139; A-293
30. Cutter ″	Grayish-black porphyritic felsite, weathers yellowish-gray	A-21/A-28; A-26; A-32; A-46; A-48; A-137; A-157
31. Cutter (variety indeterminate	Grayish-black porphyritic felsite, weathers yellowish-gray	A-17; A-54; A-85; A-87; A-88; A-89; A-93; A-103; A-125; A-188; A-278
32. Cutter (variety micro-graver)	Crystal quartz	A-134; A-216; A-283; A-353
33. Cutter (variety flaked graver)	White (milky) quartz	A-238
34. Cutter ″	Grayish-black chert, mottled, badly jointed with many vesicles	A-60; A-110 (objects are fragments of same uniface)
35. Burin	Crystal quartz	A-23; A-152; A-218; A-381

struments. Especially large flakes may have been reduced to preforms and ultimately to fluted projectile points, but this complete transformation appears never to have occurred at Adkins.

The working tool-kit of the Adkins folk may have resembled the group of more than 200 flaked stone artifacts that was deposited as grave goods or as a cenotaph at the Crowfield site in southwestern Ontario (Deller and Ellis 1984). At Crowfield a single feature yielded at least 84 bifaces, including 29 that were fluted. Next in order of abundance were large flakes or tool blanks, followed by sidescrapers and "retouched flakes."

Another burial assemblage with fluted points, in this case of the Clovis type rather than the later Crowfield type, is the Anzick site near Wilsal, Montana (Lahren and Bonnichsen 1974). Although an analysis and inventory of the full assemblage have yet to be published, it is reputed to consist of over 100 flaked stone and bone artifacts. Like Crowfield, fluted projectile points, various bifaces and utilized flakes are well represented. The Anzick find might also be a hunter's personal tool-kit of the sort members of the Adkins group might have carried with them during their travels.

While only finished implements and tool blanks (large flakes) of felsite and chert were introduced to the Adkins site, tools of crystal quartz were manufactured right on the spot. One, or perhaps two, large crystals were reduced by hammering. A hammerstone, likely used in conjunction with an anvil, must have been employed for the initial processing of this tough raw material (Callahan 1979). Since crystal quartz is anisotropic, it is easiest to remove long flakes by striking along the c-axis of the crystal, that is, from the pointed end downward. Since very few flakes discarded at the encampment show the convergent facets present at a crystal's end, originally the crystal(s) may have been singly-terminated. This observation suggests that the raw material was quarried, perhaps from a vug or pocket in one of the pegmatites that abound in western Maine and north-central New Hampshire.

By weight, crystal quartz is the third most important raw material at Adkins. Of greater importance are two dark gray to black felsites, one variety having phenocrysts (**Table 1**). All three raw materials likely originated well to the south of the Magalloway valley somewhere north and east of Lake Winnipesaukee where volcanic rocks and their close relatives are well exposed (see Chapter Two).

The four varieties of dark gray to black chert that together constitute the fourth most important class of raw materials by weight (**Table 1, varieties 5, 7, 9 and 10**) appear to be derived from outcrops in the Champlain Lake Lowland and east-central New York state. A bewildering number of cherts and chert-bearing rock formations exist in this broad region (Hammer 1976, Wray 1948). Slight differences in color, texture, inclusions and mottling serve to distinguish these various cherts, which are all gray, black or blue in color. Several of the formations with chert outcrop nearly continuously over broad areas, making it impossible to attribute tool raw materials to specific locations. The Oriskany Formation, for example, is exposed across central New York in Ontario, Seneca, Cayuga, Onondaga, Madison, Oneida and Herkimer counties (Wray *ibid*), and according to Hammer the unit extends even farther to the east as far as Albany, New York. Its line of outcrop also runs in a north-south direction from Albany to the northern New Jersey border.

A small quantity of Oriskany chert occurs at Adkins, and it is termed "grayish-black chert with quartz spherules." bearing in mind that its parent formation is a band nearly 400 km long, any effort to pinpoint a source may be futile, perhaps even misguided.

Of all the cherts that the writer has seen, the mottled dark gray and olive-gray chert at Adkins most closely resembles chert from outcrops near St. Albans, Vermont. Stone from this source, it is thought, may be represented at other New England Palaeo-Indian sites such as Michaud in south-central Maine (Spiess and Wilson 1987). The grayish-black vesicular chert, most pieces having joints, also may have originated in Vermont, but perhaps more to the south near the New York border. A source at Mt. Independence, Vermont, is known to have been exploited prehistorically, as were numerous outcrops in the vicinity of Whitehall, New York. Varieties of chert found there, conforming to Wray's descriptions of Whitehall Dolomite Flint and Fort Ann Limestone Flint, may be present in small amounts at the Vail site (Gramly 1985a: 76). These cherts were favored for the production of trianguloid endscrapers, which were often transformed into cutters and *pièces esquillées.*

Next in abundance after the cluster of gray cherts is grayish-red to dusky-red chert or silicified argillite. The source of this stone is unknown. Large glacial erratics of red argillite may be seen here and there in western Maine streambeds, and the ultimate origin of this raw material likely lies to the north in Quebec. An example is an argillite boulder in the gorge of Sandy Creek near New Sharon (Farmington region), Franklin County, Maine. The gorge is approximately 80 km to the southeast of the Adkins site. The boulder appears to have had flakes struck off it (Robert Doyle, personal communication).

Like the red chert or argillite, the white (milky) quartz at Adkins might be derived from a boulder in a streambed or deposit of glacial gravel. Massive white quartz with good fracturing properties is also common in the western Maine pegmatite district south of the Magalloway and Androscoggin Rivers in central and southern Oxford County. There, too, may be found abundant crystal quartz. Perhaps all of the milky quartz debitage at Adkins was generated by reducing a biface. A fluted point may have been manufactured although no recognizable channel flake was unearthed as proof. Fluted points of white quartz are exceedingly uncommon in northeastern North America, and milky quartz has a reputation for being a difficult material to flake. Some knappers were able to rise above this apparent handicap and produce very regular, thin fluted points (Saxon 1973: Fig. 1f).

Minority lithics in the Adkins assemblage are a grayish-red chert, a lustrous dark reddish-brown chert, a fine olive-gray quartzite, and a lineated aphanitic stone represented by a single heavy tool but no debitage. The origins of these raw materials are unknown to the writer. The grayish-red chert grades to a coarser raw material that is best described as a silicified sandstone. Stone of similar appearance was unearthed at the Whipple Palaeo-Indian site in southwestern New Hampshire (Curran 1984: 9; Curran, personal communication). The Whipple site also yielded a suite of quartzites, one of which undoubtedly originated in western Vermont (Curran and Grimes n.d.).

The greenstone hammer together with another like it that generated the flakes found at Adkins may have been plucked from glacial gravels somewhere in the immediate vicinity of the encampment.

The lithic raw materials deposited at Adkins, in sum, suggest a movement by the site's Palaeo-Indian occupants from the south or southwest. Conspicuously absent in the assemblage are stones from northern and northeastern Maine sources such as Ledge Ridge chert, the suite of Cambro-Ordovician cherts outcropping near Munsungan and

Chase Lakes in Piscataquis County (Pollock 1987), and gray-green, porphyritic felsites from Brassua and Kineo Lakes (the so-called Kineo felsites). No other fluted point site reported from New England has a lithic "profile" resembling that of Adkins. Whence the Adkins hunters began their journey that ultimately led to the Magalloway River valley can only be guessed. In this light it is interesting to note the scattered finds of fluted points in central and northern New Hampshire (Sargent 1982). A Palaeo-Indian encampment is thought to exist in the town of Georges Mills on Sunapee Lake, west-central New Hampshire, but to date only limited excavations have taken place (Howard Sargent, personal communication). The archaeological record of this broad region is imperfectly known, and it surely harbors other Palaeo-Indian remains — including perhaps the home territory of the Adkins group.

The two most important lithic raw materials in the Adkins assemblage by weight, the dark gray felsites **(Table 1)**, are altogether absent at other stations of the Magalloway Valley Palaeo-Indian Complex. Crystal quartz is sparingly represented at Upper and Lower Wheeler Dam and the Vail site. Champlain Lowland cherts resembling those at Adkins constitute a small, but significant, item in the Vail artifact assemblage. The possibility of confusing these raw materials with gray Ledge Ridge chert makes it hazardous to estimate their percentage on visual grounds alone. A minor amount of white quartz is present at Vail, like Adkins, but this stone is absent at other Magalloway Valley Palaeo-Indian Complex stations.

The Morss site assemblage appears to share none of the Adkins raw materials. Cherts from the Munsungan source, and perhaps particular varieties of Ledge Ridge chert, are the sole lithic materials at Morss. According to this observation, it might be argued that the occupants of Adkins and Morss entered the Magalloway valley from nearly opposite directions or they journeyed in opposite directions for their supply of tool material.

The Wheeler Dam sites and Vail, in a manner of speaking, have lithic assemblages that are intermediate between those belonging to Adkins and Morss. At these three encampments occur small amounts of the stones used by knappers who resided at Adkins and Morss; however, the bulk of their assemblages is Ledge Ridge chert. This highly variable stone was available in nearly inexhaustible supply along the talus slope of the Ridge itself north of Aziscohos Lake. The fact that the occupants of Adkins and Morss did not use this convenient source heavily, if at all, indicates that they may have been unaware of it. The Adkins and Morss groups likely colonized the Magalloway River valley, having spent some time in different regions before their arrival on the Magalloway. As both parties of hunters became familiar with the resources of the valley during annual caribou harvests, they may have turned to Ledge Ridge as the principal source of stone for their flaked implements.

Artifacts According to Raw Material

The most important facts to emerge from this study of the Adkins site, insofar as Palaeo-Indian behavior is concerned, are general, *viz.,* 1) the encampment was occupied only once, 2) the distribution of artifacts suggests a single structure that could have accommodated 6-8 people, 3) the size of the tool-kit is small indicating a brief occupation, and 4) the gross composition of the artifact assemblage is similar to other suites of Palaeo-Indian artifacts in the Magalloway valley and at other localities in the glaciated Northeast, implying that occupants of the various sites performed some identical acts. A fifth general fact is revealed by the raw materials used for tools. We know that the Adkins knappers obtained their stone in the south and southwest; direct visits to lithic sources may have been made.

No detailed metrical studies of artifact classes or statistical manipulations are necessary to derive the above information. The Adkins assemblage is so small that numerical analyses — routine for larger, very productive Palaeo-Indian encampments like Vail, Debert or Bull Brook — were not applied.

For the benefit of other researchers making comparative studies, however, it was decided that elementary observations about selected tools and flakes in the Adkins assemblage should be presented. Measurements (or the range of a measurement) of length and maximum width are given for most whole specimens using Gramly 1982: Figure 7 as a guide. For some analysts these few attributes will prove insufficient, and reference will have to be made to the Adkins site collection, which is housed at the Maine State Museum in Augusta.

The entire Adkins assemblage, as listed in **Table 19,** is curated by the Maine State Museum. To my knowledge this group is the full complement of objects discovered at the site. No collector is known to have kept any tool or flake from this encampment. Any specimens unearthed in future years at Adkins likewise will be deposited at the Maine State Museum.

Tools and debitage are partitioned according to their raw materials and are discussed separately. Comments about artifacts follow the order of tools and debitage presented in **Tables 4-18.** The conventional treatment of describing artifacts independently of their raw materials, or at best, appending raw material identifications as an afterthought, is abandoned here. Since the properties of stones dictate the tools that might be fashioned from them, it follows that raw material should be treated as the primary variable.

1. Dark gray, finely banded felsite, weathers light olive-gray **(Table 4)**

This felsite is the most abundant (by count and weight) raw material at the Adkins site. Being homogeneous and free of gross flaws even in large pieces, it was employed for a wide range of tools. It was brought to the camp in the form of large flakes and bifaces. Tools of this stone were resharpened on site and converted to new forms.

This felsite is presumed to outcrop somewhere in north-central New Hampshire, well to the south of the Magalloway River valley.

A single fluted point of banded felsite was unearthed. This point is short (41 mm) and narrow (maximum width 24 mm). It conforms in size to the smallest, retipped (but not radically reworked) fluted projectile points on record for the Vail site (*cf.* Gramly 1982: Plate 7a). The outline of the point is essentially straight-sided **(Plate 16),** and workmanship is mediocre. There are at least two channel flakes on each face. The maximum length of channel flake scar on each face is 22 mm and 17 mm. Grinding extends from the ears along the edges to the termination of the shorter channel flake scar. Slight grinding is present within the basal concavity. The maximum thickness of the point is 7 mm.

Despite its small size, the fluted point is still wide enough to be hafted on a thrusting spear (Gramly 1984a). Although still of some use, the point was likely culled in favor of a longer, sharper spearhead.

The largest flaked stone artifact at Adkins is a fluted point preform that broke in two during reduction **(Plates 16 and 17)**. Five flakes have been refitted to it, and perhaps most of the 59 biface reduction flakes and fragments of banded felsite are derived from this piece as well. The preform has straight sides and a flat to gently excurvate base. In outline it is identical to a slightly shorter fluted point preform recovered from the Vail site (Gramly 1982: Plate 11a). It is also reminiscent of a group of preforms reported from the Lamb Palaeo-Indian site burial, Genesee County, New York (Gramly 1987, 1988). The Adkins specimen is large (length 145 mm, width 47 mm) with a maximum thickness of 14 mm. With luck a knapper might have derived from this preform a fluted point as large as any on record for the Vail habitation site and associated kill sites. There is little doubt that the preform was destined to become a spearpoint as its edges have been dulled by an abrader in preparation for extensive flake removals.

Only one of the five sidescrapers of banded felsite is both complete and not too heavily resharpened for its original flake form to be ascertained **(Plate 18)**. It is best described as a lunate sidescraper with a curved outer margin exhibiting scraper retouch and an inner border with damage as though used as a cutter. Its maximum length is 130 mm. In both shape and size the tool recalls others known for the Potts Palaeo-Indian site, Oswego County, New York (Gramly and Lothrop 1984: Figure 8d).

TABLE 4.
Breakdown of Tools and Debitage Made of Dark Gray, Finely Banded Felsite, Weathers Light Olive-gray.*

Tools	Number
1. Fluted points	1
2. Fluted point preforms	1
3. Sidescrapers	5
4. Endscrapers	1
5. *Limaces*/groovers	2
6. *Pièces esquillées*	2
7. Cutters	12
8. Tool fragments	13
TOTAL	**37** (702.7 grams)

Debitage	Number
1. Biface reduction flakes	30
2. Uniface resharpening flakes	6
3. Scaled/splintered flakes	7
4. Flake fragments	29
5. Unidentified flakes	6
TOTAL	**78** (63.1 grams)

*Counts include tools that were transformed on site.

A flat flake with its bulb of percussion broken away was retouched into a rough trapezoidal or trianguloid form making it classifiable as an endscraper **(Plate 19).** Possibly this endscraper was retooled from a fragmentary *limace.* Its length is 45 mm and the width of the broader working end is 23 mm.

Two *limaces* or groovers fashioned of banded felsite were discovered at Adkins **(Plate 19).** The larger tool has removals on its flat ventral face, which were made in an attempt to remove the projecting bulb of percussion for hafting. Both *limaces* are long (92 mm, 68 mm) and wide (22 mm and 21 mm respectively) in comparison to the mean dimensions of *limaces* at the Vail site (Gramly 1982: Table 6). In a pristine state, not shortened by resharpening, both specimens likely exceeded the estimated upper limit of length for *limaces* (termed "flakeshavers" by Grimes and Grimes) from the Bull Brook site, Massachusetts (Grimes and Grimes 1985: 44).

An utilized flake at least 70 mm long was battered at its distal and proximal ends and served as a *pièce esquillée.* It shattered into angular chunks as a result of this hammering. One of the resulting fragments was itself used as a *pièce esquillée.* Whether *pièces esquillées* of banded felsite from Adkins are tools or cores is not easily decided. Certainly none of the removals from these felsite specimens were useful to Palaeo-Indian workers as the flakes were thin, fragile and short (under a cm in length). This observation conforms with an analysis of *pièces esquillées* from the Vail site (Lothrop and Gramly 1983). This analysis gave weight to the idea that these objects served as wedges for splitting and were not cores. The restored former utilized flake is shown in **Plate 20.**

At least 12 banded felsite cutters of the variety, utilized flakes, were discarded at the Adkins encampment. These implements are large, ranging in length from 47 mm to 113 mm with a mean of nearly 69 mm. With minimal retouching and shaping any of these flakes could have been transformed into a sidescraper or endscraper. The abundance of seemingly still serviceable cutters at Adkins raises the possibility that they were cached to be reclaimed during a future visit. One of the shorter cutters of banded felsite is shown in **Plate 19.**

Most of the 13 banded felsite tool fragments appear to belong to cutters (utilized flakes). One fragment appears to be a mid-section of an endscraper.

2. Grayish-black porphyritic felsite, weathers yellowish-gray **(Table 5)**

A basal fragment of a fluted projectile point of this raw material was discovered at Adkins. Its surviving length is 33 mm with a width of 31 mm at the break. The basal concavity is 6 mm deep, and grinding is present within the concavity as well as on both ears and cutting edges. This point was neatly fashioned with a single wide channel flake on each face **(Plates 16 and 17).** The terminations of both channel flake scars were carried away with the tip section. The distance from the basal concavity to the break is 24 mm — or well within one standard deviation of the mean for this measurement made on a group of fragmentary fluted points from Vail (Gramly 1984a). This observation suggests that fluted points from Vail and Adkins were hafted similarly, perhaps as the tips of thrusting spears.

Constituents of a single large sidescraper of porphyritic felsite were scattered about the Adkins encampment and restored to form the specimen illustrated in **Plate 20.** After breakage, perhaps intentional, part of the sidescraper continued in use as a sidescraper although it may have served briefly as a *pièce esquillée.* Another portion was employed solely as a *pièce esquillée,* and flakes as long as 15 mm were detached by crushing blows. This restored sidescraper is a fine example of how Palaeo-Indians transformed stone tools in response to needs of the moment.

A short, heavily resharpened *limace* or groover was discovered made of porhyritic felsite. This specimen is 22 mm wide at its widest point and only 44 mm long. Its ventral face at the proximal end has a few flake removals, perhaps to facilitate hafting. Resharpening has given this *limace* shoulders, which were likely absent on a fresh tool in pristine condition **(Plate 19).**

Seven cutters of the variety, utilized flakes, found at Adkins were fashioned of porphyritic felsite. Since all the tool fragments of this raw material are derived from unifaces, this total is the full count of cutters discarded by Palaeo-Indians. The cutters range in length from 49 to 71 mm, and as a group they are shorter than cutters made of banded felsite.

TABLE 5.
Breakdown of Tools and Debitage Made of Grayish-black Porphyritic Felsite, Weathers Yellowish-gray.*

Tools	Number	
1. Fluted points	1	
2. Sidescrapers	1	
3. *Limaces*/groovers	1	
4. *Pièces esquillées*	1	
5. Cutters	7	
6. Tool fragments	3	
TOTAL	**14**	191.5 grams)

Debitage	Number	
1. Biface reduction flakes	6	
2. Uniface resharpening flakes	4	
3. Scaled/splintered flakes	3	
4. Flake fragments	4	
5. Unidentified flakes	6	
6. Angular waste flakes	2	
TOTAL	**25**	(38.2 grams)

*Counts include tools that were transformed on site.

One of the cutters (A-21/A-28) was detached by a knapper from the same block of felsite as two angular waste flakes (A-98 and A-291). The three artifacts fit against one another and were struck off in consecutive blows **(Figure 14).** The angular flakes are 53 mm and 58 mm in length, falling well within the size range of cutters made of this raw material; yet, they appear never to have been used.

Both angular flakes were discovered in the presumed dump area a few meters to the west of the entrance to the Adkins tent or dwelling. As these flakes are ungainly in form with thick medial ridges, they may have been ill-suited for use and were tossed away. Actual cutters are, in general, flatter and exhibit more regular shapes. The care shown in choice of tools by the Adkins site occupants is evidence that they were well supplied with lithic raw material.

3. Crystal quartz **(Table 6)**

No bifaces of crystal quartz were discovered at Adkins, and the lack of biface reduction flakes of this raw material indicates that none were resharpened or manufactured on the spot. The crystals of optically clear quartz appear to have been too small for manufacturing fluted points, except for miniature points (possibly toys) that are recovered from time to time at Palaeo-Indian sites (*e.g.,* Moeller 1980: Plate 7 a and c).

Bipolar hammering, presumably in conjunction with an anvilstone, was the principal way quartz crystals were reduced to useful shapes. Judging by the small-sized cutters (utilized flakes) in the Adkins assemblage, any flake a centimeter or more in length was potentially useful as a tool. Homogeneous crystal quartz is a hard, tough material when it is free of flaws, and small pieces are more durable than most flakes of chert, felsite and argillite. Slivers of crystal quartz mounted in handles could easily make cuts in hard substances such as bone and antler.

Since the evidence is unequivocal that the Adkins site inhabitants used small crystal quartz flakes as tools, there is a strong case for regarding *pièces esquillées* of this raw material as cores, not tools. Yet, many specimens show no long flake scars and only battering or crushing on opposed edges. These particular *pièces esquillées* were not successful cores although they may have been effective wedges for splitting antler, wood and other substances. In sum, the Adkins *pièces esquillées* likely served as both cores and tools. Incidental flakes produced by hammering wedges surely would have been laid aside for future use as cutters.

It is interesting to observe that the Adkins knappers did not attempt to produce regular cores, blades or bladelets from crystal quartz. This material is well suited to blade production — witness its use by Dorset groups in the archaeological record of Labrador (Cox 1978). Blade cores are rare to non-existant on eastern North American fluted point sites and as Haynes notes (1980: 116), they are sometimes confused with *pièces esquillées.* A tool industry based on blades, by strict definition, is absent at Adkins and other stations of the Magalloway Valley Palaeo-Indian Complex. Blade cores also do not turn up at Palaeo-Indian lithic workshops where they might be expected in great number. Instead, blocky and irregular cores are unearthed, and flakes were struck from almost any appropriate platform (Funk 1976: 220).

The largest tool of crystal quartz discovered at Adkins is a sidescraper 48 mm long **(Plate 22)**. This implement saw hard service and is very well worn on all edges except the bulbar end.

The 12 trianguloid endscrapers from Adkins range in length from 11 mm to 29 mm, averaging only 22 mm **(Plate 21)**. As a group they are the smallest endscrapers of any from Magalloway Valley Complex sites. Being so small, special hafts with sockets

TABLE 6.
Breakdown of Tools and Debitage of Crystal Quartz.

Tools	Number	
1. Sidescrapers	1	
2. Endscrapers	12	
3. *Pièces esquillées*	16	
4. Cutters	24	
5. Burins	4	
6. Tool fragments	6	
TOTAL	**63**	(148.6 grams)

Debitage	Number	
1. Uniface resharpening flakes	4	
2. Scaled/splintered flakes and angular waste flakes	72	
3. Cores	1	
TOTAL	**77**	(36.0 grams)

or sleeves may have been necessary. The miniature endscraper (length 11 mm) recalls others reported from Locus A at the Vail site (Gramly 1985a: 91).

Sixteen *pièces esquillées* were identified among the Adkins assemblage **(Plate 23).** They range in length from 13 mm to 37 mm with a mean of 25 mm. A third of this class exhibits flake scars caused by bipolar hammering; these specimens may be cores. The others have only crushed edges and are better regarded as wedges, or failed cores. Although wedges of crystal quartz have yet to be described from any northeastern North American Palaeo-Indian site, they have been noted in an Early Archaic context at the Shawnee-Minisink site near East Stroudsburg, Pennsylvania (McNett 1977: 46).

Cutters of crystal quartz number 24. Most are simple utilized flakes **(Plate 22),** but three micro-cutters have intentionally shaped points. These tools **(Plate 22, bottom row)** would be termed gravers or graving spurs by most analysts. Absent from the Adkins assemblage are coronet gravers and other varieties with pronounced, needle-like points. The Adkins series of cutters have lengths from 8 mm to 44 mm with a mean size of 18 mm. The smaller specimens appear to have originated as scaled and splintered flakes struck off *pièces esquillées* with the exception of one micro-graver, which was fashioned from a sharp-cornered uniface resharpening flake. The use of uniface resharpening flakes for micro-gravers was also observed at the Vail site (Gramly 1985a: 91).

Three angle burins and possibly a fourth were present at the Adkins site. Planes along which the burin blows were struck meet at acute angles, and strong, sharp points were formed on the tools **(Plate 23, bottom row).** Burins of this shape are termed dihedral burins, and they have been illustrated from Palaeo-Indian and later prehistoric sites in Texas (Epstein 1961). Dihedral angle burins based on fragmentary fluted points are also known from the Nobles Pond Palaeo-Indian site (Gramly and Summers 1986: Figure 4). Gravers in combination with burins have also been described from the Gainey site in Michigan (Simons *et al.* 1984). East of Ohio, burins are rare or non-existant. The enormous flaked stone assemblage from the Bull Brook site, for example, does not feature them, and they are altogether absent at Vail. Their occurrence at Adkins may be unique among fluted point Palaeo-Indian encampments in the Northeast and may stem from the use of this special raw material — crystal quartz.

4. Grayish-red to dusky-red chert or silicified argillite **(Table 7)**

The sole identifiable tool of this raw material is a large (107 mm long) sidescraper **(Plate 18).** Both long edges of this scraper exhibit resharpening resulting in a marked taper towards the bulbar end. With additional removals the piece might have become as narrow as a *limace.*

Among the debitage is a very large biface reduction flake (47 mm long). It was struck from a thin, well-made biface at least 60 mm wide, to judge by old flaking scars on the dorsal surface of this flake. Interesting to note, the fluted point preform of banded felsite, discussed earlier, may have been this wide before it was reduced in a failed attempt to produce a spearpoint. Since there are so few biface reduction flakes of red chert or argillite, it is evident that the Palaeo-Indian knapper did not intend to manufacture a fluted point of this raw material. Rather, the knapper may have been seeking a large, sharp flake for use as a cutter. Unfortunately this large flake collapsed when it was struck and it never became a cutting tool. All the other biface reduction flakes of red chert or argillite are small, and they may have been produced when a striking platform was set up in preparation for removing the large flake. The use of large bifaces as cores has long been suspected for Palaeo-Indian flaked tool industries, and the Adkins assemblage furnishes a good example of this strategy of production.

TABLE 7.
Breakdown of Tools and Debitage made of Grayish-red to Dusky-red Chert or Silicified Argillite.

Tools	Number
1. Sidescrapers	1
2. Tool fragments	1
TOTAL	**2** (29.5 grams)

Debitage	Number
1. Biface reduction flakes	8
2. Uniface resharpening flakes	2
3. Flake fragments	1
4. Unidentified flakes	4
TOTAL	**15** (14.5 grams)

While the large bifaces carried in the tool-kit of every Palaeo-Indian group served as cores and ultimately as a source of fluted points, they also may have been effective knives or cleavers for butchering and other heavy tasks. In this regard discoveries at the Wight Palaeo-Indian site on the glacial outwash plain west of the Vail encampment take on interest. In 1984 three large fragmentary bifaces were unearthed at Wight. In addition there was found a very large biface reduction flake that had been struck from a biface other than the ones discarded at the site. This flake had been used as a cutter. No other flaked stone artifacts were encountered, even on the sieves. These facts suggest that kills were butchered at Wight. Only 130 m to the west is located Vail kill site #2 — a locus where two fluted points were discovered.

5. Mottled dark gray and olive-gray chert (**Table 8**)

The small sidescraper (length 36 mm) of this raw material is heavily worn on its dorsal surface, possibly from rubbing against a haft. Other flaked tools from Adkins exhibit similar abrasion and polishing. For the sidescraper (A-31/A-115) and other objects discovered in the lag sand, however, it is difficult to distinguish between actual

TABLE 8.
Breakdown of Tools and Debitage Made of Mottled Dark Gray and Olive-gray Chert.

Tools	Number
1. Sidescrapers	1
2. *Pièces esquillées*	1
3. Cutters	2
4. Tool fragments	1
TOTAL	**5** (34.5 gams)

Debitage	Number
1. Uniface resharpening flakes	7
2. Flake fragments	1
3. Unidentified flakes	3
TOTAL	**11** (2.0 grams)

tool wear caused by use and damage resulting from years of exposure to waves of Aziscohos Lake and other water action.

The *pièce esquillée* of dark gray and olive-gray mottled chert was formerly a trianguloid endscraper approximately 28 mm in length. Hammering on the working edge, as it stood on its proximal (bulbar) end, caused a flake to shear away the full length of the tool. This scaled and splintered flake was not discovered.

Two cutters, one 41 mm long and the other 52 mm in length, were discovered. Both are the variety, utilized flakes **(Plate 19)**.

6. Dark gray to dark yellowish-brown lineated aphanitic stone **(Table 9)**

The sole artifact of this striking raw material is a sidescraper **(Plate 20)**. This tool was once part of a larger scraper, and the sharp edge of an old break has been dulled by flaking and made more regular.

TABLE 9.
Breakdown of Tools and Debitage Made of Dark Gray to Dark Yellowish-brown Lineated Aphanitic Stone.

Tools	Number
1. Sidescrapers	1 (33.4 grams)

No debitage of this raw material was recovered.

7. Grayish-black chert with many vesicles **(Table 10)**

Two trianguloid endscrapers and perhaps a third represented by an unifacial tool fragment were fashioned from this lustrous, dark chert. The maximum length of these endscrapers is 32 mm, which is very close to the mean size (33 mm) of these tools at the Vail site (Gramly 1982: 35). It is remarkable that no resharpening flakes relating to these unifaces were recovered in the Adkins excavation, suggesting that the scrapers were at the end of their useful life when they were brought to the encampment.

An oval cutter 62 mm in length was manufactured of this chert. Both edges were heavily utilized **(Plate 19)**.

TABLE 10.
Breakdown of Tools and Debitage Made of Grayish-black Chert with Many Vesicles.

Tools	Number
1. Endscrapers	2
2. Cutters	1
3. Tool fragments	1
TOTAL	**4** (29.8 grams)

No debitage of this raw material was recovered.

8. White (milky) quartz **(Table 11)**

A biface of white quartz was reduced at the Adkins site, generating 46 flakes and flake fragments plus a small angular chunk. It may be assumed that a fluted point was made although no channel flakes were recognized among this debitage. The angular chunk was retouched to produce a diminutive cutter or graving spur **(Plate 18)**.

Tools and debitage of white quartz are scarce at all Palaeo-Indian sites in the Magalloway valley.

TABLE 11.
Breakdown of Tools and Debitage Made of White (Milky) Quartz.

Tools	Number
1. Cutters	1 (1.3 grams)

Debitage	Number
1. Biface reduction flakes	33
2. Unidentified flakes	13
TOTAL	**46** (25.0 grams)

9. Grayish-black chert with quartz spherules **(Table 12)**

Three trianguloid endscrapers and three tool fragments (two belonging to unifaces) are fashioned of this highly distinctive raw material from eastern New York state. The length of the endscrapers ranges from 27 mm to 32 mm. The proximal end of the smallest implement is rounded by retouching, and it appears to be a fragment of a slightly larger tool **(Plate 18)**.

Several uniface resharpening flakes were recovered in the excavation indicating that the endscrapers were put to use at the encampment.

TABLE 12.
Breakdown of Tools and Debitage Made of
Grayish-black Chert with Quartz Spherules.

Tools	Number
1. Endscrapers	3
2. Tool fragments	3
TOTAL	**6** (25.1 grams)

Debitage	Number
1. Uniface resharpening flakes	4
2. Unidentified flakes	1
TOTAL	**5** (.5 grams)

10. Grayish-black chert, mottled, badly jointed with many vesicles **(Table 13)**

Fragments of a tool, apparently a sidescraper or other uniface, were retouched unifacially to create two cutters of the variety, flaked gravers. Both cutters are shown joined along the initial line of fracture **(Plate 18)**. Two other cutters of this chert were based on flakes, one of which is an uniface resharpening flake.

TABLE 13.
Breakdown of Tools and Debitage Made of Varieties of
Grayish-black Chert, Mottled, Badly Jointed with Many Vesicles.*

Tools	Number
1. Cutters	4 (20.5 grams)

Debitage	Number
1. Biface reduction flakes	1
2. Uniface resharpening flakes	2
TOTAL	**3** (.4 grams)

*Counts include tools that were transformed on the site.

11. Grayish-red chert (Table 14)

A single tool, a cutter of the variety utilized flake, was fashioned of this raw material whose source is unknown (Plate 19). An uniface resharpening flake of this distinctive raw material indicates that an uniface was kept at Adkins, as well.

TABLE 14.
Breakdown of Tools and Debitage Made of Grayish-red Chert.

Tools	Number
1. Cutters	1 (4.9 grams)

Debitage	Number
1. Uniface resharpening flakes	1 (.1 grams)

12. Fine olive-gray quartzite (Table 15)

No tools of this high-quality raw material were discovered. A biface was lightly resharpened at the encampment and likely departed in the tool-bag of a hunter.

TABLE 15.
Breakdown of Tools and Debitage Made of Fine Olive-gray Quartzite.

Debitage	Number
1. Biface reduction flakes	1
2. Scaled/splintered flakes	1
3. Flake fragments	4
TOTAL	6 (.7 grams)

No tools of this raw material were recovered.

13. Lustrous dark reddish-brown chert (Table 16)

An uniface of this attractive raw material was resharpened and presumably used at the Adkins encampment without being discarded.

TABLE 16.
Breakdown of Tools and Debitage Made of Lustrous Dark Reddish-brown Chert.

Debitage	Number
1. Uniface resharpening flakes	1 (.1 gram)

No tools of this raw material were recovered.

14. Greenstone (Table 17)

A weathered, angular chunk of greenstone, comfortable for holding, was unearthed from the soils at the Adkins site. The chunk exhibits a few fresh-appearing flake scars, suggesting that it may have been used as a hammerstone by Palaeo-Indians. Similar objects, some bearing dimpling or scarring on flat surfaces, were recovered from the Vail site. They are classed as hammer-anvils in most cases (Gramly 1982: Plate 26).

The existence of another hammer-anvil at the Adkins encampment can be inferred from seven angular waste flakes in the assemblage. All are the same sort of greenstone, but it was possible to attach only two of the flakes (A-107 and A-183). These flakes record successive hard blows to a striking platform at a relatively high angle to the flake release surface — approximately 80 degrees. The parent piece was likely a blocky cobble.

TABLE 17.
Breakdown of Tools and Debitage of Greenstone.

Tools	Number
1. Hammerstones	1 (510 grams)

Debitage	Number
1. Angular waste flakes	7 (85.6 grams)

None of the seven angular waste flakes was sharpened to make a tool, and there is no evidence visible to the naked eye that they were employed as cutters.

Percussion tools of rough, grainy stone are regularly encountered at northeastern North American Palaeo-Indian sites (*cf.* MacDonald 1968: 104-107 for a discussion), and the Magalloway Valley Palaeo-Indian Complex sites are no exceptions. Use of the flakes that were the incidental result of hammering with these implements appears to have been infrequent and followed no set pattern. The writer has yet to discover a formal tool such as a trianguloid endscraper or lunate sidescraper fashioned from a flake of coarse, grainy stone that was struck off an hammer-anvil.

15. Unidentified raw materials (**Table 18**)

A small fragment of an uniface made of nondescript gray stone, perhaps a felsite or chert, could not be assigned to any of the 14 recognized categories of raw materials. A pot-lidded flake of similar stone was also unearthed.

Finally, a very badly weathered angular waste flake of what seems to be coarse felsite, now tan in color, was sieved from the lag sand. Tan, buff and flesh-colored felsites (rhyolites) may be seen at outcrop in central New Hampshire (Lalish 1979), while closer to the Adkins site in northwest Maine and the upper Magalloway valley dark gray to light gray felsites predominate. Bearing in mind that the specimen from Adkins is severely weathered and its color may not be true to fresh rock at outcrop, a New Hampshire origin for the artifact is favored.

TABLE 18.
Breakdown of Tools and Debitage Made of
Unidentified Raw Materials.

Tools	Number
1. Tool fragments	1 (.6 grams)

Debitage	Number
1. Angular waste flakes	1
2. Pot-lidded flakes	1
TOTAL	**2** (1.9 grams)

Summary of Evidence, Interpretations and Speculations

The Adkins site is important to archaeological science because of its unique character and to culture history for what it has to say about ancient human behavior.

To archaeologists it is a rare example of a relatively unmolested Palaeo-Indian encampment that is mercifully free of mixing with artifacts of later periods. The archaeological deposit has great integrity and it is intimately associated with a stone feature. This unique feature is the oldest standing construction in eastern North America.

What makes the Adkins site worthy of our attention is its close relationship to other sites of the same cultural phase in one mountain valley. Adkins is not just an isolated encampment, rather, it belongs to an archaeological complex. Much is already known about other members of the Magalloway Valley Palaeo-Indian Complex; these insights advance our understanding of the occupation of Adkins itself.

In both areal extent and the size of its artifact assemblage Adkins is small. It is dwarfed by the Vail encampment with its thousands of chert tools, including hundreds of fluted points and fluted drills. Yet, in terms of behavior the Adkins and Vail sites are much the same. Identical stone implements in roughly the same proportions were used and deposited at both encampments.

In the Magalloway valley "major" sites like Vail are the sum of many "minor" sites like Adkins. Repeated occupations over many years, perhaps generations, by hunting parties or small family units sharing a single tent would be required to generate the thick carpet of lithic debris that was left behind at Vail.

The reason(s) why Palaeo-Indians occupied some sites in the Magalloway valley but once, like Adkins, and others repeatedly is open to speculation. The explanation may be of small importance for appreciating regional prehistory. Even the concept, "Magalloway Valley Palaeo-Indian Complex," proposed here may be a low-level construct, which is relevant to interior northern Maine and New Hampshire only.

Undoubtedly many such Palaeo-Indian site complexes could be defined in northeastern North America. A dependable food supply is surely one of the reasons why Palaeo-Indian sites are found clustered. For the Magalloway valley, we have argued that excellent caribou hunting was a primary attraction. A similar explanation might be invoked to account for clusters of Palaeo-Indian sites across south-central Ontario (*cf.* Storck 1982).

Another reason why sites might be clumped is the exploitation of geographically limited lithic resources of superior grade. A good example of a group of Palaeo-Indian sites that is linked to a regionally important lithic source is the Flint Run Complex of northern Virginia (Gardner 1983), and many other examples could be cited (*e.g.,* Lepper, n.d.).

Formulating archaeological complexes is a necessary step towards defining archaeological cultures, which are high-level, intricate intellectual constructs. To date no archaeologist has attempted to define a Palaeo-Indian culture for northeastern North America. A reluctance to do so stems from a lack of information about mortuary patterns, diet, and non-lithic material culture. Data distilled from scores of future archaeological investigations will be required to meet this worthy goal.

Although the role of the Adkins site is limited when seen from the grand perspective of archaeological science, the site provides priceless testimony about human behavior during the remote era when eastern North America was first settled. The events that transpired in the Magalloway valley had been acted out similarly a thousand times before in other, formerly glaciated regions.

We may infer that ten to eleven thousand years ago a groupof 6-8 Palaeo-Indians, perhaps a single family, arrived in the Upper Magalloway valley. This exploratory party may have set out on their journey to the western Maine highlands from the hills flanking the White Mountains of New Hampshire. There they had lately procured divers raw materials for tool-making, including felsite, argillite and perhaps crystal quartz. In addition, the group carried in their tool-bags a few implements fashioned of lustrous cherts from sources in the west near Lake Champlain.

It cannot be known at this late date what prompted the group to trek northward 100-150 kilometers. Competition for limited dependable food supplies, heightened by local declines in the abundance of caribou, may have spurred these people to seek a better lot elsewhere. Also, this exodus could have been prompted by cultural factors, such as death of a close family member, which may have required survivors to abandon their home to the ghost of the deceased.

The hunters likely timed their move to coincide with the spring migration of caribou. They followed on the heels of herds headed for calving grounds among the meadows, mountains and snowfields along the international boundary between Canada and the United States. Well worn animal trails were easy routes for human movement and led hunters directly to their quarry.

Palaeo-Indians kept to the trail as far north as the Narrows of the upper Magalloway valley. Here was a superb place to intercept caribou during their return migration in fall. At this point the valley was hemmed in by steep ledge, and passing herds would be forced to keep to the valley floor while running a gauntlet of spears wielded by skilled hunters.

Camp was made on the eastern side of the valley among rocks and ground-hugging vegetation covering a low rise or ridge. The small settlement was completely exposed to a strong wind blowing on most days from the northwest. Although the wind could be cold and drive people indoors from time to time, it was nevertheless welcome as it helped dissipate clouds of tormenting flies and mosquitoes. More importantly, the wind carried away human scent from the sensitive noses of wary game.

Water and firewood were obtainable along the sheltered course of Lincoln Brook, which flowed a few hundred meters south of the encampment. Little else was needed from the surrounding countryside as a Palaeo-Indian group on the move was prepared for almost any contingency and was well furnished with tools, clothing, and construction materials for making shelters. Such a load could be conveyed easily on a sled drawn by dogs and assisted through difficult places by drivers. The hides used to cover a tent framework alone weighed scores of kilograms — a great burden for the back of any man. An alternative conveyance for transporting heavy household gear and food was the toboggan together with snowshoes for crossing deep snowdrifts that persisted in the Maine highlands until late spring.

With skill honed by a lifetime of practice the Palaeo-Indians pitched a hide tent and secured it well against the wind. There were abundant rocks close at hand to weight down the skirt. Only a few wooden poles supported the covering, but a space five meters in diameter was created — sufficient room for the group to sleep and work in comfort.

The tent door was positioned facing west towards the direction caribou herds were expected to appear. Outside and to the right of the door was a favored sitting place for adults. Here was room to spread out tools and raw materials, and a watch for caribou in the valley could be kept, too.

During the long, anxious wait for returning herds, the Adkins Palaeo-Indians busied themselves in preparation for the hunt. New fluted point speartips were flaked from large bifaces that every hunter carried in a tool-bag. Spear shafts and other impedimenta were made using stone scrapers and cutters. Craftsmen sorted among their supplies of sharp stone flakes looking for the one of the right size and shape suited to the task at hand. Occasionally fresh flakes were struck off bifacial cores. Gradually broken tools and flakes resulting from tool maintenance and manufacture carpeted the area just inside the door of the tent where most work was done. Some of this litter was swept towards the rear of the tent or tossed outside along with other refuse.

While waiting for the hunt to begin, members of the group may have fished. The Magalloway River, which flowed close at hand, held many trout. Fish were good food for dogs and human beings alike.

At last the caribou arrived. Either they passed by in great numbers or were uncommonly tame, for the Adkins hunters were able to amass more meat than they could consume or even carry away. The valley had not been hunted in many years, perhaps not ever. There was an abundant supply of meat, fat, antler for toolmaking, sinew, and hides. The hides were particularly valuable as they were in top condition and the perfect thickness for making into clothing.

With so much excess meat, it was decided to erect a store or cache. A shallow pit was dug at the base of large boulders a few meters outside the door of the tent. Other large rocks were dragged to the edge of the pit and arranged so as to overjut slightly, creating an open-topped chamber. Smaller rocks were wedged around the big ones to prevent scavengers like foxes from entering and eating the meat. A roof of poles and rock slabs was devised to span the gap in the center of the structure, and when a heavy doorstone was rolled into place and wedged tightly, the cache was secure against all intruders. The 10-14 deboned caribou carcasses inside were welcome insurance against times of scarcity. Knowing that a meat supply was safely stored away, the Adkins group may have decided to explore the Magalloway valley before returning to their winter quarters in the south.

Perhaps during this first season of exploration the Adkins Palaeo-Indians chanced upon Ledge Ridge and its plentiful supplies of chert, which was well-suited for knapping into tools. One thing is certain: they ceased using dark gray felsites, argillites and kindred raw materials for their implements.

After that first year the Adkins site was not occupied again. Other places along the east side of the valley were selected for camping. Insofar as it is known, these spots all lie north of the Adkins site but are still strategically situated near the Narrows. The names given to these encampments are Cox, Vail and Morss. Only the Vail site has evidence of repeated occupations over many years. West of these sites was the favored killing ground used by Palaeo-Indians; there lie Vail kill sites #1 and #2 and at least one place where animals may have been dismembered (Wight site).

A few kilometers north of the Magalloway valley meadows on a former bank of the Little Magalloway River are two additional Palaeo-Indian encampments. They are situated at another good place for intercepting southward-moving animals. Judging by the flaked stone tools that were unearthed at these stations (Upper Wheeler Dam and Lower Wheeler Dam), they may have been inhabited by the Adkins Palaeo-Indians years after they first entered the Magalloway region or possibly by their descendants.

Since the assemblages of stone artifacts at all the Palaeo-Indian sites in the upper Magalloway valley are so similar in style and content, they may be lumped as a single cultural complex. It cannot be inferred on the basis of this construct that human occupation during the era when fluted points were manufactured in the Magalloway valley was continuous and closed to outside influences. In fact, radical differences in the types of stone used by occupants of the Adkins and Morss sites for their implements suggest that the valley was entered and perhaps resettled from different directions. Since the principal quarry of the Magalloway band, it is felt, was caribou, human occupation must have moved in step with the changing activity of the caribou herds. This species suffers occasional declines and will abandon portions of its accustomed range; so, Palaeo-Indian hunters must have quit the Magalloway River region from time to time.

Ever so slowly the archaeologist's trowel has begun to lay bare the prehistory of the Palaeo-Indian inhabitants of northwestern Maine. In speculating upon the lifestyles and fortunes of the Magalloway band, we begin to relive an exciting era. It was a time of stepping out into unexplored lands and of coping with unknown challenges. From a perspective of nearly 11,000 years we can find reasons to envy these colonizers of a New World, and as we handle their shapely tools crafted of selected raw materials, the pride of their former owners is almost tangible, almost real.

References Cited

Boas, Franz
    1884   The Central Eskimo. *Annual Report (Sixth) of the Bureau of Ethnology,* pp. 409-667. Washington.
Bombard, Carole J. and Ronald B. Davis
    1985   A temporal vegetation continuum: From tundra to forest. *Explorations* 1(2): 18-21. University of Maine. Orono.
Bonnichsen, Robson
    1985   Anatomy of an excavation. *Explorations* 1(2): 22-28. University of Maine. Orono.
Bonnichsen, R., V. Konrad, V. Clay, T. Gibson and D. Schnurrenberger
    1980   Archaeological research at Munsungan Lake: 1980 preliminary technical report of activities. Institute of Quaternary Studies, University of Maine. Orono.
Bowers, Peter M., Robson Bonnichsen, and David M. Hoch
    1983   Flake dispersal experiments: Noncultural transformations of the archaeological record. *American Antiquity* 48(3): 553-572.
Burch, Ernest S., Jr.
    1971   The caribou/wild reindeer as a human resource. *American Antiquity* 37(3): 339-368.

Callahan, Errett
 1979 The basics of biface knapping in the Eastern Fluted Point Tradition: A manual for flintknappers and lithic analysts. *Archaeology of Eastern North America* 7(1): 1-179.

Cox, Steven L.
 1978 Palaeo-Eskimo occupations of the North Labrador coast. *Arctic Anthropology* 15(2): 96-118.

Curran, Mary Lou
 1984 The Whipple site and Paleoindian tool assemblage variation: A comparison of intrasite structuring. *Archaeology of Eastern North America* 12: 5-40.

Curran, Mary Lou and John R. Grimes
 n.d. Paleoindian exploitation of coastal environments in the Western Gulf of Maine: Comments on Oldale. Paper presented at the Spring 1987 meeting, Northeastern Anthropological Association. Ms. in possession of authors.

Deller, D. Brian and C. J. Ellis
 1984 Crowfield: A preliminary report on a probable Paleo-Indian cremation in southwestern Ontario. *Archaeology of Eastern North America* 12: 41-71.
 n.d. Early Paleo-Indian complexes in Southwestern Ontario. Paper delivered at the Smith Symposium, Buffalo Museum of Science, Buffalo, New York. October, 1986.

Doyle, Richard A., Nathan D. Hamilton, James B. Petersen and David Sanger
 1985 Late Paleo-Indian remains from Maine and their correlations in Northeastern prehistory. *Archaeology of Eastern North America* 13: 1-34.

Ellis, Christopher John
 1984 Paleo-Indian Lithic Technological Structure and Organization in the Lower Great Lakes Area: A First Approximation. Doctoral dissertation (unpublished). Department of Anthropology, Simon Fraser University. Burnaby.

Epstein, Jeremiah F.
 1961 Burins from Texas. *American Antiquity* 26(1): 93-87.

Fitting, James E.
 1975 *The Archaeology of Michigan.* Cranbrook Institute of Science. Bloomfield Hills, Michigan.

Fitting, James E., Jerry DeVisscher and Edward J. Wahla
 1966 The Paleo-Indian Occupation of the Holcombe Beach. *Anthropological Papers, Museum of Anthropology, University of Michigan* 27. Ann Arbor.

Freuchen, Peter and Finn Salomonsen
 1958 *The Arctic Year.* G. P. Putnam. New York.

Funk, Robert E.
 1976 Recent Contributions to Hudson Valley Prehistory. *New York State Museum Memoir* 22. Albany.

Gardner, William M.
 1983 Stop me if you've heard this one before: The Flint Run Paleoindian Complex revisted. *Archaeology of Eastern North America* 11: 49-64.

Gramly, Richard Michael
 1980 Prehistoric industry at the Mt. Jasper mine, northern New Hampshire. *Man in the Northeast* 20: 1-24.
 1982 The Vail Site: A Palaeo-Indian Encampment in Maine. *Bulletin of the Buffalo Society of Natural Sciences* 30. Buffalo, New York.

1984a Kill sites, killing ground and fluted points from the Vail site. *Archaeology of Eastern North America* 12: 110-121.

1984b Mount Jasper: A direct access lithic source area in the White Mountains of New Hampshire. Pp. 11-22 *in* Jonathon E. Ericson and Barbara A. Purdy (eds.) *Prehistoric Quarries and Lithic Production.* Cambridge University Press.

1985a *Recherches archéologiques au site paléoindien de Vail, dans le nord-ouest du Maine,* 1980-1983. *Recherches Amérindiennes au Québec* 15 (1-2): 57-118.

1985b Report on Archaeological Survey, Salvage Excavations and Reconnaissance in Oxford and Franklin Counties, Me. Report (129 pp.) on file with the Maine Historic Preservation Commission, Augusta, Maine.

1987 An unique fluted point site in western New York. *Indian Artifact Magazine* 6(1): 4-6. Turbotville, Pennsylvania.

1988 Palaeo-Indian sites south of Lake Ontario, western and central New York state. Pp. 125-145 *in* R. S. Laub, N. Miller, and D. W. Steadman (eds.) Late Pleistocene and Early Holocene Paleoecology and Archaeology of the Eastern Great Lakes Region. *Buffalo Society of Natural Sciences Bulletin* 34. Buffalo, New York.

Gramly, Richard Michael and Jonathan Lothrop
1984 Archaeological investigations of the Potts site, Oswego County, New York, 1982 and 1983. *Archaeology of Eastern North America* 12: 122-158.

Gramly, Richard Michael and Kerry W. F. Rutledge
1982 Molls Rock: A multi-component site in northern New Hampshire. *Man in the Northeast* 24: 121-134.

Gramly, Richard Michael and Garry L. Summers
1986 Nobles Pond: A fluted point site in northeastern Ohio. *Midcontinental Journal of Archaeology* 11(1): 97-124.

Grimes, John R. and Beth G. Grimes
1985 Flakeshavers: Morphometric, functional and life-cycle analyses of a Paleoindian unifacial tool class. *Archaeology of Eastern North American* 13: 33-57.

Grimes, John R., W. Eldridge, B. G. Grimes, A. Vaccaro, F. Vaccaro, J. Vaccaro, N. Vaccaro and A. Orsini
1984 Bull Brook II. *Archaeology of Eastern North America* 12: 159-183.

Hammer, John
1976 Identification and distribution of some lithic raw materials from New York state. *Man in the Northeast* 11: 39-62.

Haury, Emil W., E. B. Sayles, and William W. Wasley
1959 The Lehner mammoth site, southeastern Arizona. *American Antiquity* 25(1): 1-30.

Hawkes, E. W.
1916 The Labrador Eskimo. *Canada Geological Survey Memoir* 91(14). Ottawa.

Haynes, C. Vance
1980 The Clovis culture. *Canadian Journal of Anthropology* 1(1): 115-21.

Hoffman, Curtiss
1985 Revising the Late Archaic period in southern New England. *Archaeology of Eastern North America* 13: 58-78.

Jenness, Diamond
1928 *The People of the Twilight.* Macmillan Company. New York.
Lahren, Larry and Robson Bonnichsen
1974 Bone foreshafts from a Clovis burial in southwestern Montana. *Science* 186: 147-150.
Lalish, Beth G.
1979 The Petrography of Archaeological Materials in New Hampshire. Report on file, Department of Anthropology, University of New Hampshire. Durham.
Lepper, Bradley T.
n.d. Early Paleo-Indian land use patterns in the central Muskingum River basin, Coshocton County, Ohio. Paper presented at Midwestern Archaeological Conference, Columbus, Ohio, October, 1986.
Loring, Stephen
1980 Paleo-Indian hunters and the Champlain Sea: A presumed association. *Man in the Northeast* 19: 15-42.
Lothrop, Jonathan C. and Richard Michael Gramly
1983 *Pièces esquillées* from the Vail site. *Archaeology of Eastern North America* 10: 1-11.
MacDonald, George F.
1968 Debert: A Paleo-Indian Site in Central Nova Scotia. *National Museum of Canada Anthropology Papers* 16. Ottawa.
McCary, Ben C.
1951 A workshop site of Early Man in Dinwiddie County, Virginia. *American Antiquity* 18(1): 9-17.
McNett, Charles W. Jr.
1977 The Upper Delaware valley Early Man project. *National Geographic Society Research Reports* (1977 Projects): 39-51.
Meltzer, David J.
1984 On stone procurement and settlement mobility in eastern fluted point groups. *North American Archaeologist* 6(1): 1-24.
Meltzer, David J. and Bruce D. Smith
1986 Paleoindian and Early Archaic subsistence strategies in Eastern North America. Pp. 3-31 *in* Sarah W. Neusius (ed.) Foraging, Collecting and Harvesting: Archaic Period Subsistence and Settlement in the Eastern Woodlands. *Center for Archaeological Investigations Occasional Paper* 6. Southern Illinois University. Carbondale.
Moeller, Roger W.
1980 6LF21: A Paleo-Indian Site in Western Connecticut. *American Indian Archaeological Institute Occasional Paper* 2. Washington, Connecticut.
1984 Regional implications of the Templeton site for Paleo-Indian lithic procurement and utilization. *North American Archaeologist* 5(3): 235-246.
Moorehead, Warren K.
1922 *A Report on the Archaeology of Maine.* Andover Press. Andover, Massachusetts.
1931 *The Merrimack Archaeological Project.* Peabody Museum. Salem, Massachusetts.

Nicholas, George Peter III

1981 Crystal quartz as a northern New England lithic resource. Pp. 117-122 in Russell J. Barber (ed.) *Quartz Technology in Prehistoric New England.* Institute for Conservation Archaeology, Peabody Museum, Harvard University.

Palmer, Ralph S.

1954 *The Mammal Guide.* Doubleday and Company. Garden City, New York.

Pinette, Richard E.

1986 *Northwoods Echoes.* Privately printed. Berlin, New Hampshire.

Pollock, Stephen G.

1987 Chert formation in an Ordovician volcanic arc. *Journal of Sedimentary Petrology* 57(1): 75-87.

Rasmussen, Knud

1927 *Across Arctic America.* G. P. Putnam and Sons. New York.

Rich, Louise Dickinson

1942 *We Took to the Woods.* J. B. Lippincott Co. Philadelphia.

Ritchie, William A. and Robert E. Funk

1973 Aboriginal Settlement Patterns in the Northeast. *New York State Museum and Science Service Memoir* 20. Albany.

Roberts, Arthur

1984 Paleo Indian on the north shore of Lake Ontario. *Archaeology of Eastern North America* 12: 248-265.

Sargent, Howard

1982 Compilation of fluted points of eastern North America by count and distribution: An AENA project. Section on New Hampshire. *Archaeology of Eastern North America* 10: 43.

Saxon, Walter

1973 The Paleo-Indian on Long Island. *New York State Archeological Association Bulletin* 57: 1-10.

Simons, Donald B., Michael J. Shott, and Henry T. Wright

1984 The Gainey site: Variability in a Great Lakes Paleo-Indian assemblage. *Archaeology of Eastern North America* 12: 266-279.

Spiess, Arthur E.

1979 *Reindeer and Caribou Hunters.* Academic Press. New York.

Spiess, Arthur and Deborah Brush Wilson

1987 Michaud: A Paleoindian Site in the New England Maritimes Region. *Occasional Publications in Maine Archaeology* 6. Maine Historic Preservation Commission and Maine Archaeological Society. Augusta.

Spiess, Arthur E., Mary Lou Curran, and John R. Grimes

1984 Caribou (*Rangifer tarandus* L.) bones from New England Paleoindian sites. *North American Archaeologist* 6(2): 145-160.

Stephens, C. A.

1874 *The Young Moose Hunters.* Harry L. Shepard and Company. Boston.

Storck, Peter L.

1982 Paleo-Indian settlement patterns associated with the strandline of glacial Lake Algonquin in southcentral Ontario. *Canadian Journal of Archaeology* 6: 1-31.

Thostrup, C. B.

    1917   Ethnographic description of the Eskimo settlements and stone remains in North-east Greenland. *Meddelelser om Gronland* XLIV. Copenhagen.

Wight, Eric

    1985   *Maine Game Wardens.* DeLorme Publishing Company. Freeport, Maine.

Wing, Lawrence A. and Arthur J. Dawson

    1949   Preliminary report on asbestos and associated rocks of northwestern Maine. Pp. 30-62 in *Report of the State Geologist, 1947-48.* Maine Development Commission. Augusta, Maine.

Witthoft, John

    1952   A Paleo-Indian Site in Eastern Pennsylvania: An Early Hunting Culture. *Proceedings of the American Philosophical Society* 96(4): 464-495.

Wray, Charles Foster

    1948   Varieties and sources of flint found in New York state. *Pennsylvania Archaeologist* 18(1-2): 25-45.

Index*

Bone artifacts 22
Bonnichsen, Robson 7, 22, 39, 42
Bourque, Bruce iv, 3, 16, **96**
Bowers, Peter M. 13, 39
Bowers, Wynn iv
Brassua Lake 24
Brown Company 5
Buffalo Museum of Science iv, 2, 3, **102**
Bull Brook phase 10
Bull Brook site, Mass. 25, 27, 30, **56**
Burch, Ernest S., Jr. 10, 16, 39
Burial assemblage 22
Burial chambers (Inuit) 15
Burins 11, 17, **21, 29,** 30, **110, 112, 114, 115, 118**
Burin blow 30

C-zone (of podzol) **64, 65**
Caches 11, 16, 38, **74**
Caches (of tools) 20, 27
Callahan, Errett 22, 40
Calving grounds of caribou 10, 37
Cambro-Ordovician cherts 7, 23
Canada 37
Caribou (forest-dwelling) 8
Caribou bone (in archaeological deposits) 8
Caribou Eskimo 16
Cayuga Co., N.Y. 22
Cenotaph 22
Ceramic Period (in Maine) 1, 9, 10
Champlain Lake Lowland 7, 22, 24
Channel flakes 3, 10, 25, 26, 27, 32
Chase Lake 24
Clay, V. 39
Clothing 8, 10, 37, 38
Clovis 22
Cold weather tent (of Inuit) **102**
Colonizers 39
Conjoined flaked stone artifacts 13, **19,** 20, **20, 21, 72, 73, 80, 81**
Connecticut **56**
Cores 27, 29, **29,** 30, 31, 38, **110, 115**
Coronet flaked gravers 17, 30
Cox, C. D. iv, 3
Cox site, Me. 3, 8, 9, 11, 14, 38, **60, 86**
Cox, Steven L. 29, 40
Crowfield site, Ontario 22, **56**
Crystal axis 22
Crystal quartz 7, **18-21,** 22, 23, 24, 28, **29,** 30, 37, **108, 110**

Vaccaro brothers 41
Vail site, Me. (see also Loci A and H) 1, 2, 3, 7-14, 17, 18, 20, 23-27, 30, 31, 32, 34, 36, 38, **60, 78, 86, 100**
Vail kill site #1, Me. 1, 2, 9, 10, 20, 26, 31, 38, **60, 100**
Vail kill site #2, Me. 2, 9, 10, 20, 26, 31, 38, **60**
Vermont 7, 23
Vesicles **18, 19, 21,** 32, **32,** 33, **33, 106**
Virginia 7, 36, **56**
Volcanic rocks 7, 22

Wahla, Edward J. 40
Wasley, William W. 41
Waste flakes 12, 13, **80**
Water supply 9
Wayne, Me. 7
Weather cycles 6, 7
Wedges 27, 29, 30
Weight of artifact assemblage (Adkins site) 13, 17, **18,** 22, 24, 25, **26, 28**
West Athens Hill site, N.Y. 10, 18, **56**
Whipple site, N.H. 8, 23, **56**
White Mountains 7, 37
White (milky) quartz 9, **18,** 19, **19, 21,** 23, 24, 32, **33, 106**
Whitehall, N.Y. 23
Whitehall Dolomite Flint 23
Wight, Eric 1, 2, 8, 31, 44, **96**
Wight site, Me. 2, 9, 11, 38, **60**
Williamson site, Va. **56**
Willows 8, 9
Wilsal, Montana 22
Wilson, Deborah Brush iv, 23, 43
Wilsons Mills, Me. 5, **90**
Wing, Lawrence A. 7, 44
Witthoft, John 10, 44
Wood 18, 29
Woodward, Susan iv
Wolverines 16
Work area 13, 14, **76, 77**
Work station 13
Working tool-kit 20, 22
Wray, Charles Foster 22, 23, 44
Wright, Henry T. 43

6LF21 site, Conn. 14, **56**

*Page numbers in boldface refer to Tables, Figures and Plates; other numbers refer to text.

FIGURES 1-14

Figure 1. Map of northeastern North America showing locations of Palaeo-Indian sites and site complexes referenced in the text. 1, Debert, Nova Scotia; 2, Munsugan Lake site complex, Maine; 3, Magalloway Valley Palaeo-Indian Complex; 4, Dam site, Maine; 5, Michaud, Maine; 6, Bull Brook, Massachusetts; 7, Whipple, New Hampshire; 8, Georges Mills, New Hampshire; 9, 6LF21 (Templeton site), Connecticut; 10, West Athens Hill, New York; 11, Shawnee-Minisink, Pennsylvania; 12, Potts, New York; 13, Lamb, New York; 14, Nobles Pond, Ohio; 15, Williamson, Virginia; 16, Gainey, Michigan; 17, Holcombe, Michigan; 18, Crowfield, Ontario; 19, Thedford II, Ontario; 20, Shoop, Pennsylvania.

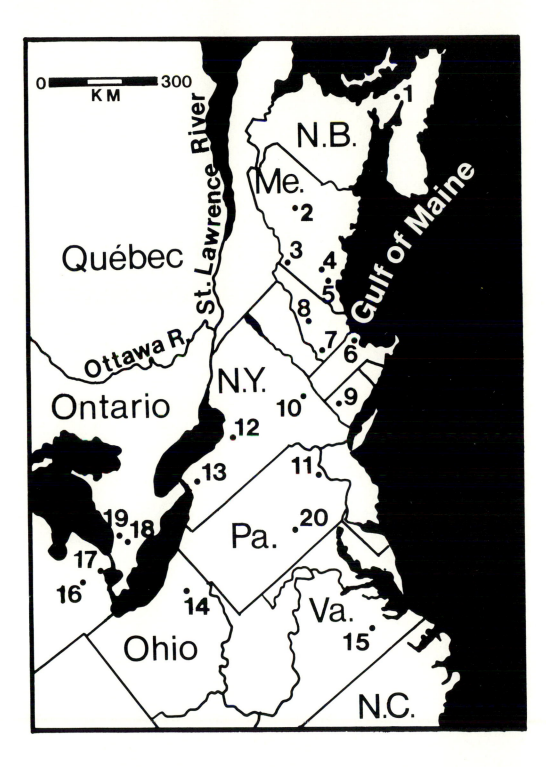

Figure 2.   1861 map of the upper reaches of the Magalloway River with additions.

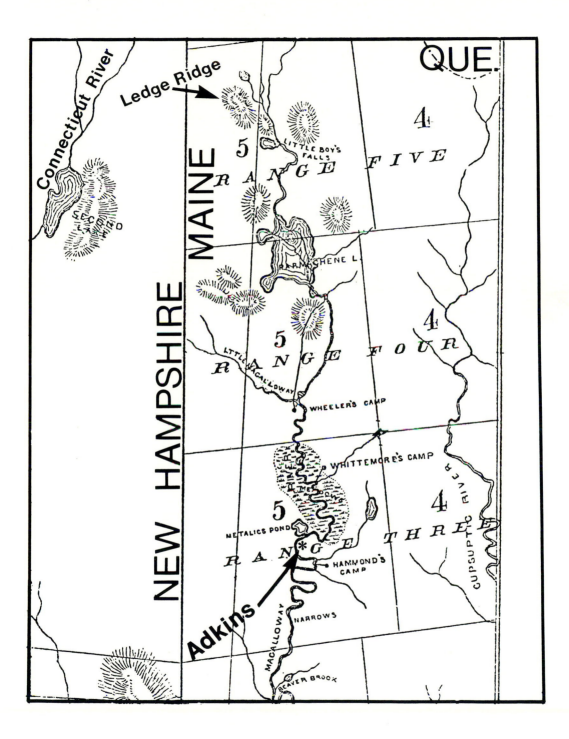

Figure 3. Map of a section of the Magalloway River valley based on an aerial photograph taken on November 4, 1984. Aziscohos Lake had completely disappeared revealing the modern Magalloway River channel, tributary streams and Metallac's Pond. Dotted areas mark glacial outwash at a level of five meters or more above the river. Dashed line traces an ancient channel of the Magalloway River, presumed to have been active during the Palaeo-Indian era.

Archaeological sites, as follows: **a,** Adkins; **b,** Vail; **c,** Vail kill site #1; **d,** Cox; **e,** Vail kill site #2; **f,** Morss; **g,** Wight.

The distance between the Vail and Adkins sites is approximately one kilometer.

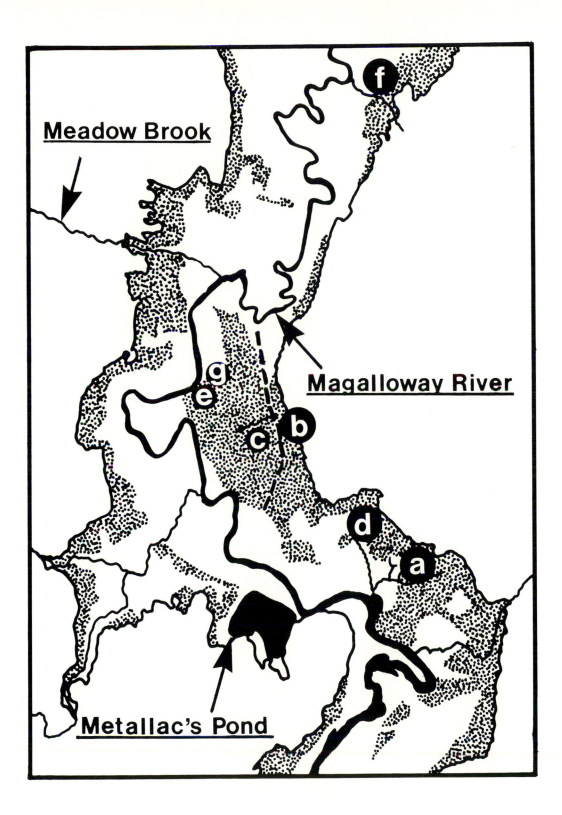

Meadow Brook

Magalloway River

Metallac's Pond

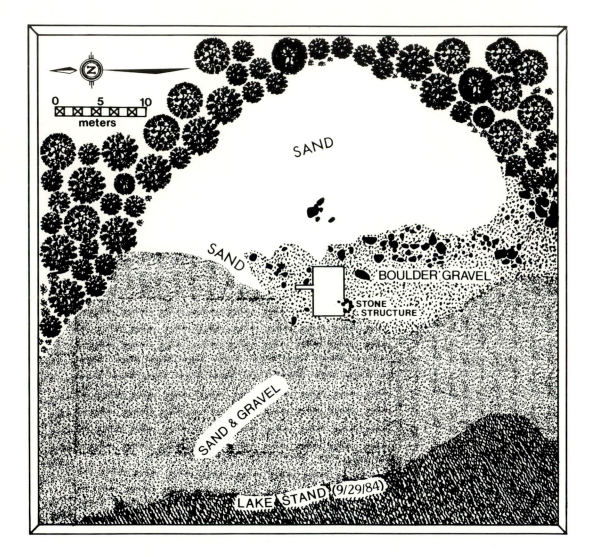

Figure 4. Map of the Adkins site at a period of low water level of Aziscohos Lake (9/29/84). The outline of the excavated area is shown.

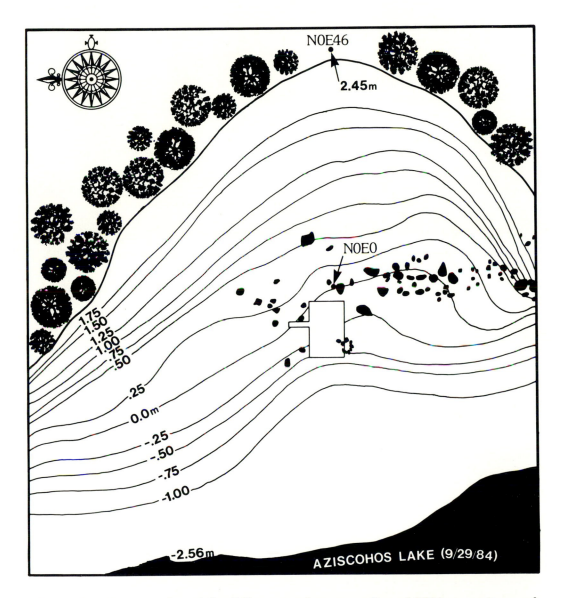

Figure 5. Contour map of the Adkins site showing outline of 1984 excavation and level of Aziscohos Lake on September 29, 1984. The normal highwater mark of the lake is marked by the tree-line. Gridpoints N0E46 and N0E0 are permanent markers. Contour interval is 25 cm.

Figure 6.   Outline of Adkins site excavations showing mapped soil units, viz., humus, A_2-zone of podzol, iron-enriched B-zone of podzol, and underlying C-zone or parent material (glacial outwash) upon which the podzol was developed.

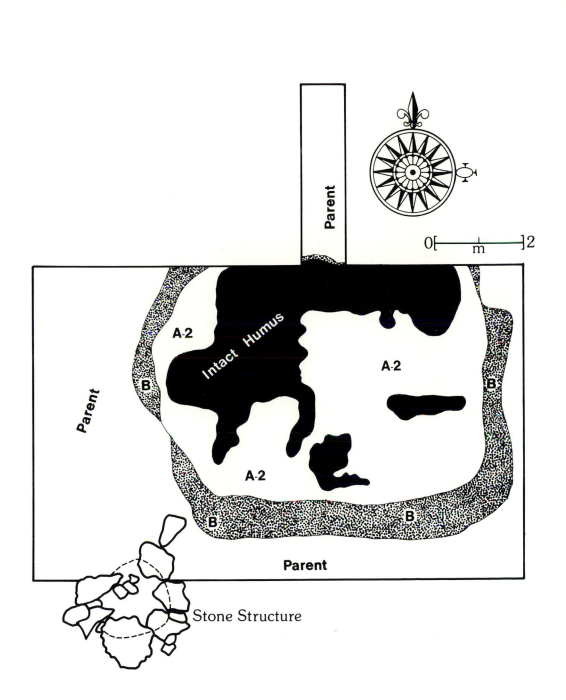

Parent

Parent

Parent

Parent

A-2

A-2

A-2

Intact Humus

B

B

B

B

0 2
m

Stone Structure

Figure 7.   Outline of Adkins site excavation showing the find-spots of 66 stone artifacts that were recovered *in situ* within forest soil. The field catalogue number of each artifact is given (See inventory, Table 19). Shaded area demarcates surviving humus and A_2-zone of forest soil.

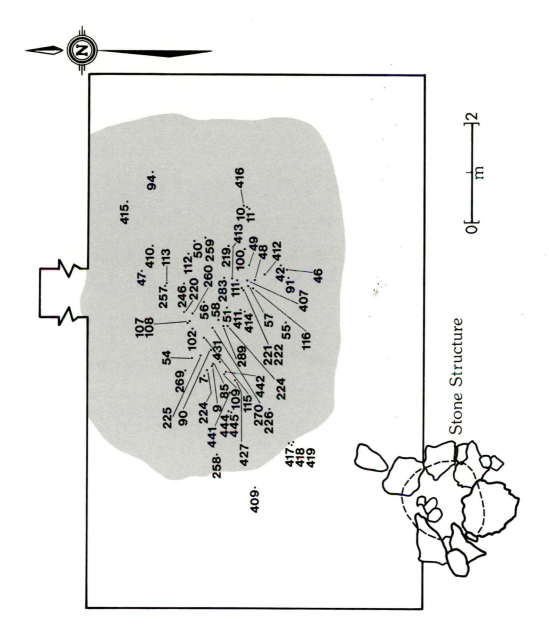

Stone Structure

Figure 8. Outline of the Adkins site excavation showing find-spots of 78 stone artifacts that were recovered in position within eroded (lag) sands. The field catalogue number of each artifact is given (See inventory, Table 19). Shaded area demarcates surviving humus and A_2-zone of forest soil.

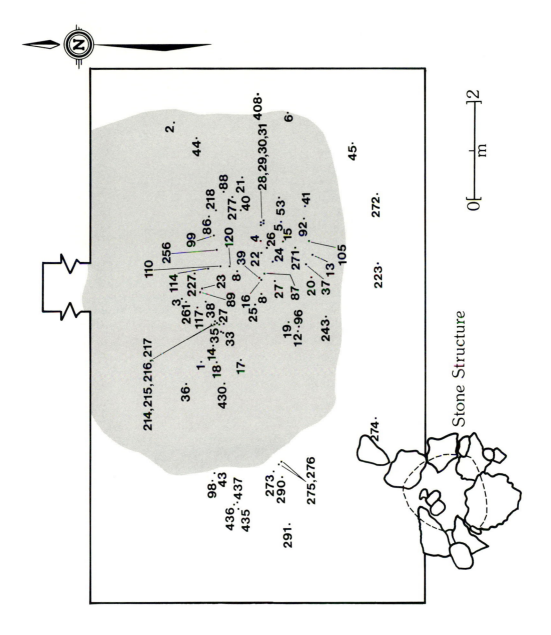

Stone Structure

Figure 9.   Outline of Adkins site excavation showing units of excavation (one-meter and two-meter squares) and tallies of artifacts recovered by sieving these units. Numbers to left of commas are tallies from sieved eroded (lag) sands; numbers to right of commas are tallies from sieved forest soil.

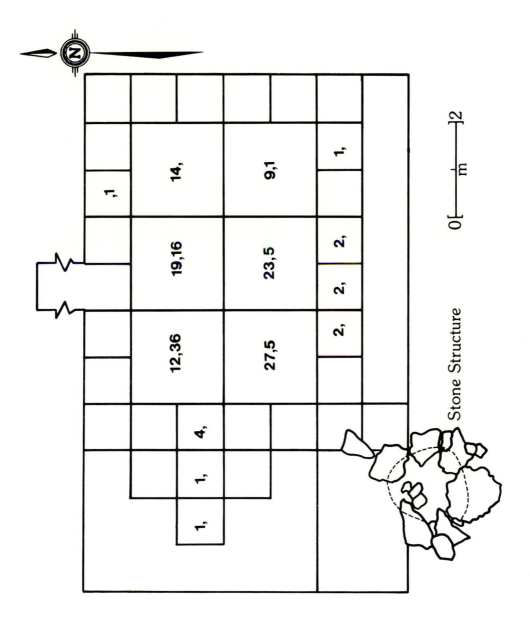

Stone Structure

Figure 10. Outline of Adkins site excavation showing the find-spots of all stone artifacts that were recovered *in situ* within forest soil and in position within eroded (lag) sands. Lines connect conjoinable artifacts.

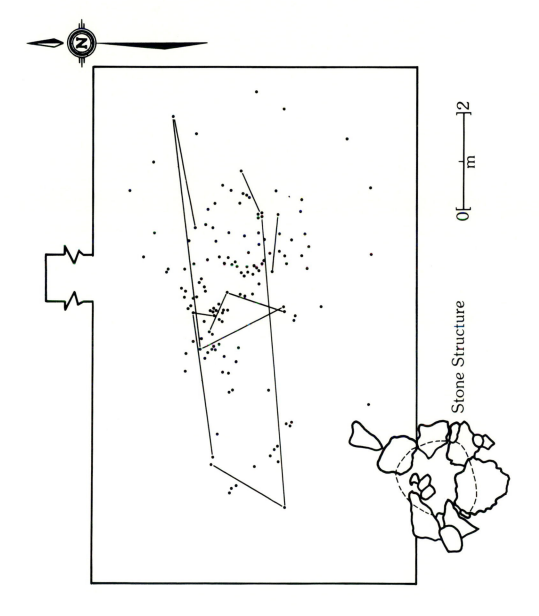

Stone Structure

0 ⌐ m ⌐ 2

Figure 11.   Plan view and cross-section of cache or permanent meat store, Adkins site, dimensions as follows: A = 1.88 m; B = 1.2 m; C = 34 cm; D = 22 cm. Average dimensions for cache are: A = 1.55 m; B = 1.05 m; C = 30 cm; D = 22 cm. The pit was excavated anciently into glacial outwash; it afterwards became partly filled with clayey, gray soil. This deposit was, in turn, covered by lag sand resulting from lakeshore erosion.

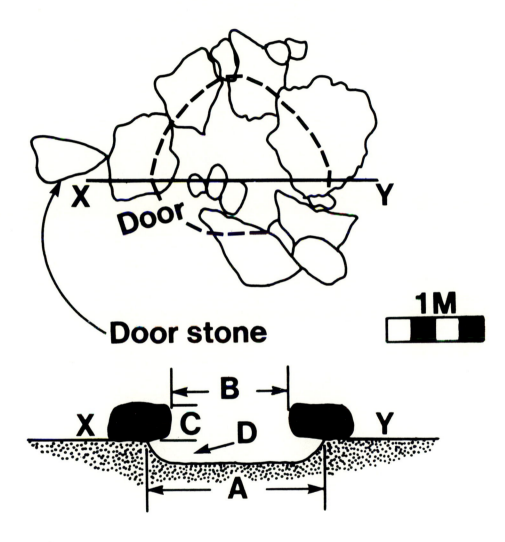

Door stone

1M

Figure 12.   Conjectured Palaeo-Indian activity areas at Adkins. It is hypothesized that the bed area of the Adkins dwelling could accommodate at least seven adults. The work area would have been heavily trafficked by occupants leaving and entering the dwelling.

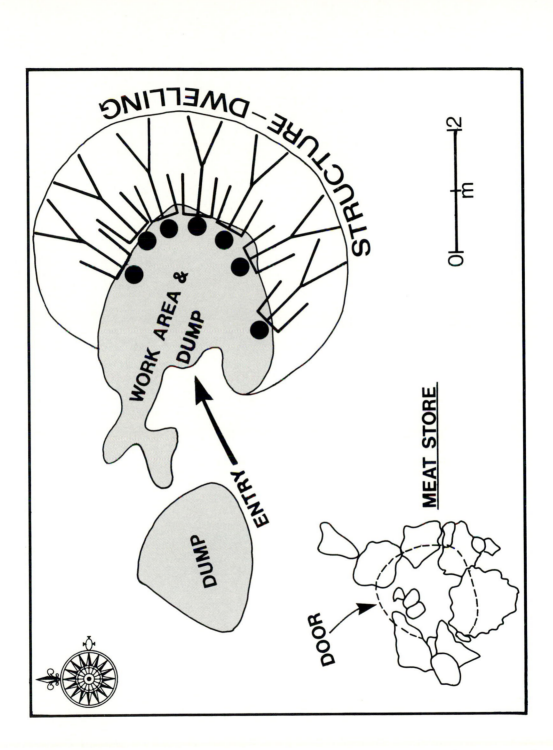

STRUCTURE-DWELLING

WORK AREA & DUMP

DUMP

ENTRY

MEAT STORE

DOOR

0 m 2

Figure 13.   Generalized map of the upper reaches of Aziscohos Lake (Magalloway River valley) showing locations of Magalloway Valley Palaeo-Indian Complex sites and from which directions lithic raw materials may have come. 1, Adkins site; 2, Vail site; 3, Morss site; 4 and 5, Wheeler Dam sites. Size of arrow is proportionate to quantity of raw material in assemblage.

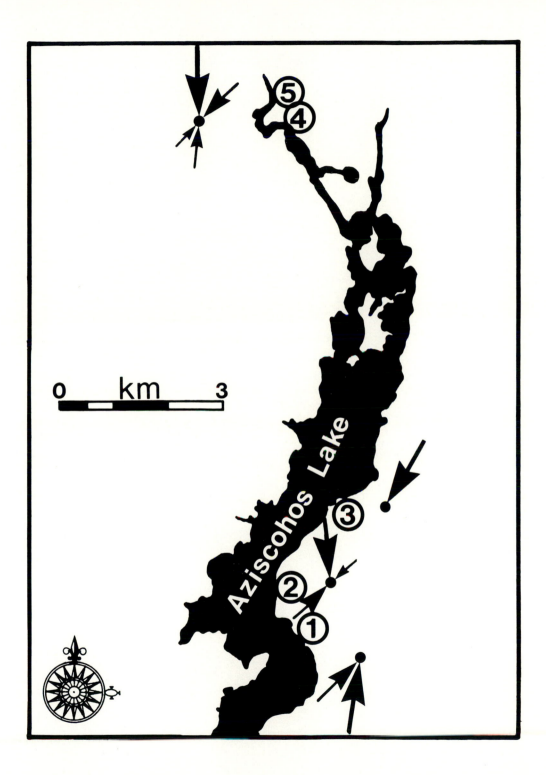

Figure 14.   **A and b,** angular waste flakes (A-98 and A-291) and **c,** a cutter (A-21/A-28), that fit against one another and were knapped from the same block of porphyritic felsite. The ventral and dorsal sides of the group of joined flakes are shown. "b" indicates bulbar end.

The waste flakes were discarded in a dump west of the Adkins dwelling site while the thinner cutter was found broken in two on the presumed floor of the dwelling. The waste flakes appear to have been too thick and irregularly shaped for use as cutters.

Shown actual size.

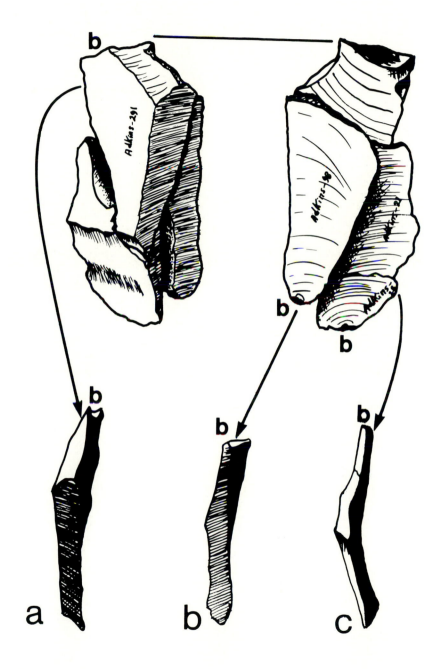

a b c

PLATES 1-23

Plate 1.   1955 aerial photograph showing the middle reaches of Aziscohos Lake and its S-shaped basin. The location of the Adkins site at the Narrows is indicated (x).

Plate 2. Aerial view of Aziscohos Lake at the Narrows with its concentration of Palaeo-Indian sites. Palaeo-Indian habitation sites are indicated by arrows: **a,** Adkins site; **b,** Cox site; **c,** Vail site; **d,** Morss site. Following the lake shore by the most direct route, it is approximately 1400 meters from the Vail encampment to Adkins.

Photo was taken in October, 1984, by R. M. Gramly on a flight piloted by Dave Heasley, Errol, New Hampshire.

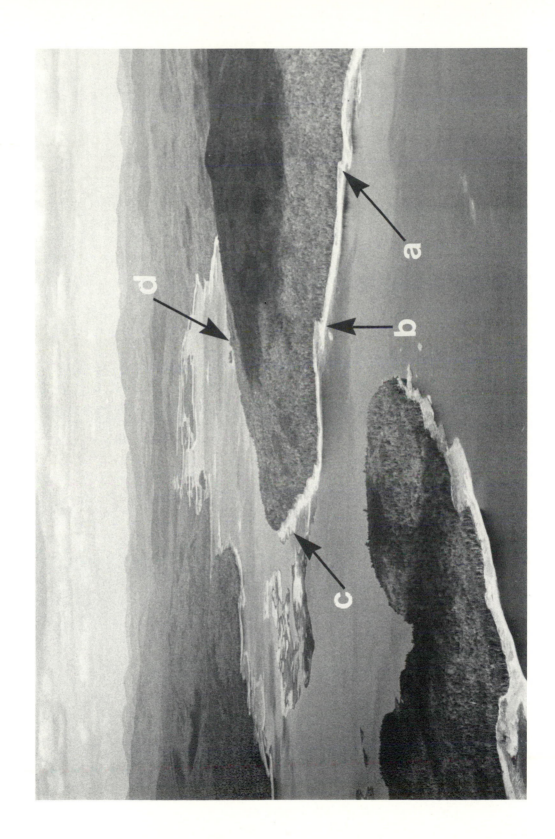

Plate 3.   Aerial view of a section of the eastern shore of Aziscohos Lake showing the cove where the Adkins site is located. Arrows indicate excavations and top opening to stone structure. Photo was taken in October, 1984, by R. M. Gramly on a flight piloted by Dave Heasley, Errol, New Hampshire.

Plate 4.   Aziscohos Dam, Wilson Mills, Maine. The dam was erected in 1909-1911 at the head of Aziscohos Falls on the Magalloway River. Until the 1950's rafts of pulp logs were hauled to the dam by steamboat and sent downstream by means of a chute (on right, partially obscured by trees). Photo by R. M. Gramly.

Plate 5.   View of Adkins site looking west on the day of discovery, September 16, 1984. Level of Aziscohos Lake is approximately eight feet below full basin level. Photo by Alexandra Morss.

Plate 6. View of the Adkins site looking east on the day of discovery, September 16, 1984. Charles Adkins is shown within the heart of the Palaeo-Indian artifact concentration, later to be excavated. Photo by Alexandra Morss.

Plate 7. View of lag sand and gravel with scattered flaked stone artifacts on the day of discovery of the Adkins site. Only four of the 16 visible artifacts are identified: **a**, sidescraper (A-4); **b**, cutter (A-15); **c**, cutter (A-22); and **d**, cutter (A-26). Photo by Alexandra Morss.

Plate 8.   Adkins site, September, 1984. Figure kneels at presumed side entrance to stone structure with possible doorstone (large rounded boulder) to the left rear and partly obscured by his left arm. Excavators in background are exploring the artifact concentration. Photo by R. M. Gramly.

Plate 9.   Adkins site stone structure before removal of washed-in sand. Photo by R. M. Gramly.

Plate 10.   Stone structure, Adkins site, November, 1984. A heavy boulder is being rolled onto a cargo net connected to a waiting helicopter. Shown moving the boulder are (from left): Junior Poor, Dr. Bruce Bourque, Warden Eric Wright and Warden Charles Adkins with Maine National Guardsmen standing by. Photo by Greg Hart, Maine State Museum.

Plate 11.   A load of boulders from the Adkins site stone structure being airlifted to Aziscohos Dam for transferral to the Maine State Museum. Photo by Greg Hart, Maine State Museum.

Plate 12.   View of 1985 excavations at the Adkins site, looking north. Students from Bates College and other volunteer amateur archaeologists are shown sieving spoil earth from the 1984 excavation through fine mesh sieves. The stone structure has been removed. Photo by R. M. Gramly.

Plate 13.   Selected fluted points from sites of the Magalloway Valley Palaeo-Indian Complex. **α** (A-3) and **b** (A-7), Adkins site; **c** (UWD-2), Upper Wheeler Dam site; **d** (V. 5582/10787), Vail habitation site (base) and Vail kill site #1 (tip); **e** (V. 5578), Vail kill site #1; **f** (LWD-24), Lower Wheeler Dam site; **g** (M. 307), Morss site; **h** (V. 3019), Vail habitation site.

　　b, c, e and **g** are extreme examples of retipping and resharpening. All specimens are slightly less than actual size.

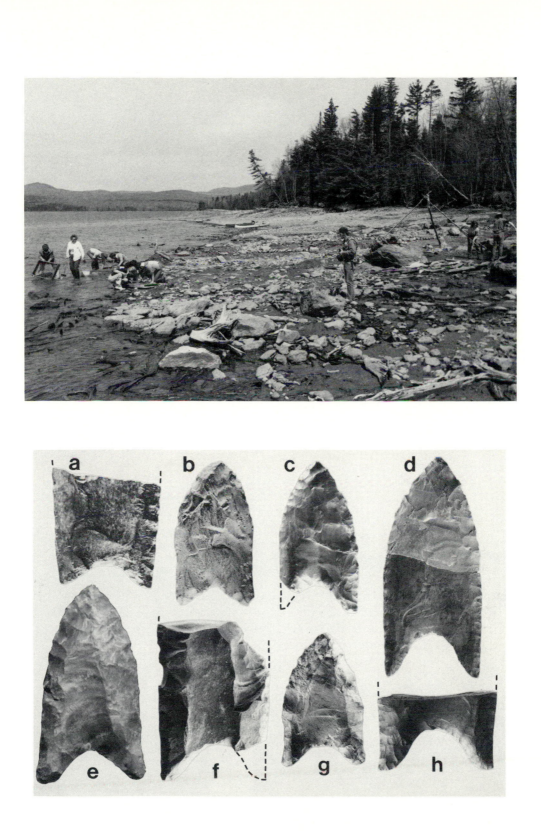

Plate 14.   Eskimo (Inuit) summer tent pieced together from caribou and seal hides. Covering appears to be supported by interior framework of one or two poles only. Area under cover appears to be roughly circular. Note boulders used to anchor edges.

Photographed at Etah, Greenland, by D. B. MacMillan in the period 1913-1925. MacMillan negative number 230549. Photo courtesy of the Buffalo Society of Natural Sciences.

Plate 15.   Eskimo (Inuit) cold weather tent pitched on an ice floe. Covering appears to be polar bear skins and caribou hides with hair on.

Photographed during 1927 Streeter Expedition to Greenland. Photo courtesy of the Buffalo Society of Natural Sciences.

Plate 16.   Fluted point preform of dark gray, finely banded felsite (A-1 and A-2) with refitted flakes (A-50, A-55, A-78, A-169 and A-317 — A-50 showing this side); fragmentary fluted point (A-3) of grayish-black porphyritic felsite; heavily resharpened, complete fluted point (A-7) of dark gray, finely banded felsite. Plates 16-23 by PRSC.

Plate 17.   Reverse of Plate 16. Refitted flakes A-55, A-78, A-169 and A-317 are seen attached to the fluted point preform.

Plate 18.   **Top row.** Trianguloid endscraper (A-61) of grayish-black chert with quartz spherules, produced from a tool fragment — chert is weathered a lighter color; sidescraper (A-4) of grayish-red to dusky-red chert or silicified argillite; large sidescraper (A-5/A-27/A-374) of dark gray, finely banded felsite.

   Bottom row. Two rejoined cutters (flaked gravers) based on fragments of an uniface (A-60/A-110) of grayish-black chert with mottlings, vesicles and joints; cutter or flaked graver (A-238) of white quartz.

Plate 19.   **Top row.** *Limaces*/groovers made of dark gray, finely banded felsite (from left, A-10 and A-6) and grayish-black porphyritic felsite (A-18); endscraper (A-92) made on possible *limace*/groover fragment of dark gray, finely banded felsite.

   Bottom row. Cutters (utilized flakes) of various raw materials: from left, mottled dark gray and olive-gray chert (A-44); dark gray, finely-banded felsite (A-139); grayish-red chert (A-186); grayish-black chert with many vesicles (A-42); and mottled dark gray and olive-gray chert (A-37).

Plate 20.   **Top.** Fragmented and restored sidescraper of grayish-black porphyritic felsite that has in part weathered to a yellowish-gray color. After breakage a portion of the tool (A-43) continued life as a sidescraper with some flake removals generated during use as a *pièce esquillée* (?); another fragment (A-288) became a *pièce esquillée.* (A-43/A-102/A-208/A-214/A-288).

   Bottom left. Former cutter or utilized flake that underwent heavy bipolar hammering and shattered. It is a *pièce esquillée.* One fragment (A-19) itself was used as *pièce esquillée.* The restored artifact is made of dark gray, finely-banded felsite. (A-19/A-51/A-90/A-121/A-173).

   Bottom right. Sidescraper (A-25) of dark gray to dark yellowish-brown lineated aphanitic stone.

Plate 21.   Selected trianguloid endscrapers of crystal quartz. (**Top row.** A-223, A-319, A-154, A-274 and A-271. **Bottom row.** A-248, A-282, A-277 and A-9).

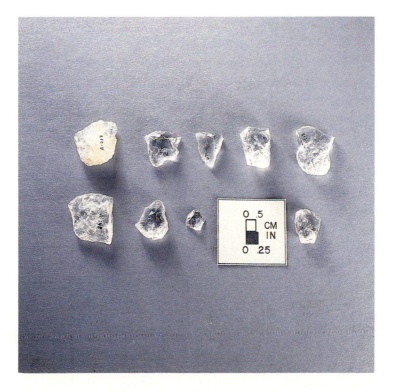

Plate 22.   Artifacts of crystal quartz.

Top row. Cutters or utilized flakes, many retaining facets of the original crystal (from left, A-8, A-304, A-13, A-150, A-339 and A-64).

Bottom row, from left. Sidescraper (A-24), cutters or microgravers (A-134, A-283, A-216 and A-353), core (A-222).

Plate 23.   Artifacts of crystal quartz.

Top row. *Pièces esquillées* (from left, A-14, A-411, A-180, A-315, A-202, A-201, A-81 and A-257)

Middle row. *Pièces esquillées* (from left, A-241, A-279, A-269, A-362 and A-246).

Bottom row. Burins (from left, A-23, A-152, A-218 and A-381).

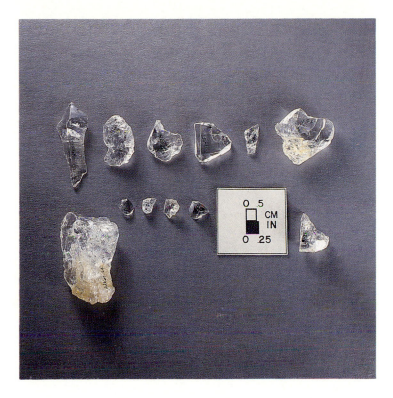

TABLE 19.
Inventory of Flaked Stone Artifacts from All Units
of Excavation at the Adkins Site.

Catalogue No.	Artifact Type	Provenance	Matching Items
1. A-1	fluted point preform fragment	*in situ*, lag sand	A-2, A-50, A-55, A-78, A-169, A-317.
2. A-2	fluted point preform fragment	*in situ*, lag sand	A-1, A-50, A-55, A-78, A-169, A-317.
3. A-3	fluted point	*in situ*, lag sand.	
4. A-4	sidescraper	*in situ*, lag sand.	
5. A-5	sidescraper fragment	*in situ*, lag sand	A-27, A-374.
6. A-6	*limace*/groover	*in situ*, lag sand.	
7. A-7	fluted point	*in situ*, soils.	
8. A-8	cutter (util. flake)	*in situ*, lag sand.	
9. A-9	trianguloid endscraper	*in situ*, soils.	
10. A-10	*limace*/groover	*in situ*, soils.	
11. A-11	AWF/SSF*	*in situ*, soils.	
12. A-12	cutter (util. flake)	*in situ*, lag sand.	
13. A-13	cutter (util. flake)	*in situ*, lag sand.	
14. A-14	*pièce esquillée*	*in situ*, lag sand.	
15. A-15	cutter (util. flake)	*in situ*, lag sand.	
16. A-16	cutter (util. flake)	*in situ*, lag sand.	
17. A-17	tool fragment	*in situ*, lag sand.	
18. A-18	*limace*/groover	*in situ*, lag sand.	
19. A-19	*pièce esquillée*	*in situ*, lag sand	A-51, A-90, A-121, A-173.
20. A-20	cutter (util. flake)	*in situ*, lag sand.	
21. A-21	cutter (util. flake) fragment	*in situ*, lag sand	A-28.
22. A-22	cutter (util. flake)	*in situ*, lag sand.	
23. A-23	burin	*in situ*, lag sand.	
24. A-24	sidescraper	*in situ*, lag sand.	
25. A-25	sidescraper	*in situ*, lag sand.	
26. A-26	cutter (util. flake)	*in situ*, lag sand.	
27. A-27	sidescraper	*in situ*, lag sand	A-5, A-374.
28. A-28	cutter fragment	*in situ*, lag sand	A-21.
29. A-29	flake fragment	*in situ*, lag sand.	
30. A-30	sidescraper	*in situ*, lag sand.	
31. A-31	cutter (util. flake) fragment	*in situ*, lag sand	A-115.
32. A-32	cutter (util. flake)	sieve, lag sand.	
33. A-33	tool fragment	*in situ*, lag sand.	
34. A-34	cutter (util. flake)	sieve, lag sand	A-49.
35. A-35	cutter (util. flake)	*in situ*, lag sand.	
36. A-36	tool fragment	*in situ*, lag sand.	
37. A-37	cutter (util. flake) fragment	*in situ*, lag sand	A-95.
38. A-38	Unidentified flake	*in situ*, lag sand.	
39. A-39	BRF*	*in situ*, lag sand.	
40. A-40	BRF	*in situ*, lag sand.	
41. A-41	AWF/SSF	*in situ*, lag sand.	
42. A-42	cutter (util. flake)	*in situ*, soils.	
43. A-43	sidescraper fragment	*in situ*, lag sand	A-102, A-208, A-214, A-288.
44. A-44	cutter (util. flake)	*in situ*, lag sand.	
45. A-45	cutter (util. flake)	*in situ*, lag sand.	
46. A-46	cutter (util. flake)	*in situ*, soils.	
47. A-47	sidescraper	*in situ*, soils.	
48. A-48	cutter (util. flake) fragment	*in situ*, soils.	
49. A-49	cutter (util. flake)	*in situ*, soils	A-34.
50. A-50	BRF	*in situ*, soils	A-1, A-2, A-55, A-78, A-169, A-317.
51. A-51	*pièce esquillée* fragment	*in situ*, soils	A-19, A-90, A-121, A-173.
52. A-52	AWF	*in situ*, lag sand.	
53. A-53	BRF	*in situ*, lag sand.	

54.	A-54	tool fragment	*in situ*, soils.	
55.	A-55	BRF	*in situ*, soils	A-1, A-2, A-51, A-78, A-169, A-317.
56.	A-56	SSF fragment	*in situ*, soils	A-171.
57.	A-57	SSF	*in situ*, soils.	
58.	A-58	*pièce esquillée*	*in situ*, soils.	
59.	A-59	cutter (util. flake)	sieve, lag sand.	
60.	A-60	cutter (flaked graver) fragment	sieve, lag sand	A-110.
61.	A-61	trianguloid endscraper	sieve, lag sand.	
62.	A-62	URF*	sieve, lag sand.	
63.	A-63	flake fragment	sieve, lag sand.	
64.	A-64	cutter (util. flake)	sieve, lag sand.	
65.	A-65	flake fragment	sieve, lag sand.	
66.	A-66	BRF	sieve, lag sand	A-298.
67.	A-67	flake fragment	sieve, lag sand.	
68.	A-68	flake fragment	sieve, lag sand.	
69.	A-69	BRF	sieve, lag sand	A-236.
70.	A-70	flake fragment	sieve, lag sand.	
71.	A-71	BRF	sieve, lag sand.	
72.	A-72	may not be an artifact	sieve, lag sand	Unplotted.
73.	A-73	BRF	sieve, lag sand	A-160.
74.	A-74	flake fragment	sieve, lag sand.	
75.	A-75	---		
76.	A-76	flake fragment	sieve, lag sand.	
77.	A-77	unidentified flake	sieve, lag sand.	
78.	A-78	BRF	sieve, lag sand	A-1, A-2, A-50, A-55, A-169, A-317.
79.	A-79	unidentified flake	sieve, lag sand.	
80.	A-80	BRF	sieve, lag sand.	
81.	A-81	*pièce esquillée*	sieve, lag sand.	
82.	A-82	AWF/SSF	sieve, lag sand.	
83.	A-83	cutter (util. flake)	sieve, lag sand.	
84.	A-84	flake fragment	sieve, lag sand.	
85.	A-85	tool fragment	*in situ*, soils.	
86.	A-86	flake fragment	*in situ*, lag sand.	
87.	A-87	tool fragment	*in situ*, lag sand.	
88.	A-88	tool fragment	*in situ*, lag sand.	
89.	A-89	tool fragment	*in situ*, lag sand.	
90.	A-90	*pièce esquillée* fragment	*in situ*, soils	A-19, A-51, A-121, A-173.
91.	A-91	hammerstone	*in situ*, soils.	
92.	A-92	trianguloid endscraper	*in situ*, lag sand.	
93.	A-93	tool fragment	*in situ*, soils.	
94.	A-94	flake fragment	*in situ*, soils.	
95.	A-95	cutter (util. flake) fragment	*in situ*, lag sand	A-37.
96.	A-96	---		
97.	A-97	---		
98.	A-98	AWF	*in situ*, lag sand	A-291.
99.	A-99	SSF	*in situ*, lag sand.	
100.	A-100	tool fragment	*in situ*, soils.	
101.	A-101	BRF	sieve, soils.	
102.	A-102	URF	*in situ*, soils	A-43, A-208, A-214, A-288.
103.	A-103	tool fragment	sieve, lag sand.	
104.	A-104	---		
105.	A-105	tool fragment	*in situ*, lag sand.	
106.	A-106	cutter (util. flake)	sieve, lag sand.	
107.	A-107	AWF	*in situ*, soils	A-183.
108.	A-108	AWF/SSF	*in situ*, soils.	
109.	A-109	URF	*in situ*, soils.	
110.	A-110	cutter (flaked graver) fragment	*in situ*, lag sand	A-60.
111.	A-111	unidentified flake	*in situ*, soils.	
112.	A-112	BRF fragment	*in situ*, soils	A-135.

113.	A-113	URF	*in situ,* soils.	
114.	A-114	unidentified flake	*in situ,* lag sand.	
115.	A-115	cutter (util. flake)	*in situ,* soils	A-31.
116.	A-116	BRF	*in situ,* soils.	
117.	A-117	tool fragment	*in situ,* lag sand.	
118.	A-118	cutter (util. flake)	sieve, lag sand.	
119.	A-119	BRF	sieve, lag sand.	
120.	A-120	flake fragment	*in situ,* lag sand.	
121.	A-121	*pièce esquillée* fragment	sieve, lag sand	A-19, A-51, A-90, A-173.
122.	A-122	BRF	sieve, lag sand.	
123.	A-123	BRF	sieve, lag sand.	
124.	A-124	SSF	sieve, lag sand.	
125.	A-125	tool fragment	sieve, lag sand.	
126.	A-126	flake fragment	sieve, lag sand.	
127.	A-127	flake fragment	sieve, lag sand.	
128.	A-128	URF	sieve, lag sand.	
129.	A-129	BRF	sieve, lag sand.	
130.	A-130	BRF	sieve, lag sand.	
131.	A-131	BRF	sieve, lag sand.	
132.	A-132	BRF	sieve, lag sand.	
133.	A-133	AWF/SSF	sieve, lag sand.	
134.	A-134	cutter (micro-graver)	sieve, lag sand.	
135.	A-135	BRF fragment	sieve, lag sand	A-112.
136.	A-136	cutter (util. flake)	sieve, lag sand.	
137.	A-137	cutter (util. flake)	sieve, lag sand.	
138.	A-138	URF	sieve, lag sand.	
139.	A-139	cutter (util. flake)	sieve, lag sand.	
140.	A-140	flake fragment	sieve, lag sand.	
141.	A-141	BRF	sieve, lag sand.	
142.	A-142	SSF	sieve, lag sand.	
143.	A-143	BRF	sieve, lag sand.	
144.	A-144	BRF	sieve, lag sand.	
145.	A-145	BRF	sieve, lag sand.	
146.	A-146	BRF	sieve, lag sand.	
147.	A-147	BRF	sieve, lag sand.	
148.	A-148	unidentified flake	sieve, lag sand.	
149.	A-149	URF	sieve, lag sand.	
150.	A-150	cutter (util. flake)	sieve, lag sand.	
151.	A-151	cutter (util. flake)	sieve, lag sand.	
152.	A-152	burin	sieve, lag sand.	
153.	A-153	tool fragment	sieve, lag sand.	
154.	A-154	trianguloid endscraper	sieve, lag sand.	
155.	A-155	BRF	sieve, lag sand.	
156.	A-156	AWF/SSF	sieve, lag sand.	
157.	A-157	cutter (util. flake)	sieve, lag sand.	
158.	A-158	SSF	sieve, lag sand.	
159.	A-159	URF	sieve, lag sand.	
160.	A-160	BRF fragment	sieve, lag sand	A-73.
161.	A-161	URF	sieve, lag sand.	
162.	A-162	BRF	sieve, lag sand.	
163.	A-163	AWF/SSF	sieve, lag sand.	
164.	A-164	flake fragment	sieve, lag sand.	
165.	A-165	flake fragment	sieve, lag sand.	
166.	A-166	unidentified flake	sieve, lag sand.	
167.	A-167	URF	sieve, lag sand.	
168.	A-168	AWF	sieve, lag sand.	
169.	A-169	BRF	sieve, lag sand	A-1, A-2, A-50, A-55, A-78, A-317.
170.	A-170	flake fragment	sieve, lag sand.	
171.	A-171	SSF	sieve, lag sand	A-56.
172.	A-172	cutter (util. flake)	sieve, lag sand.	
173.	A-173	*pièce esquillée* fragment	sieve, lag sand	A-19, A-51, A-90, A-121.
174.	A-174	AWF/SSF	sieve, lag sand.	

175.	A-175	BRF	sieve, lag sand.	
176.	A-176	BRF	sieve, lag sand.	
177.	A-177	SSF fragment	sieve, lag sand	A-178.
178.	A-178	SSF fragment	sieve, lag sand	A-177.
179.	A-179	AWF/SSF	sieve, lag sand.	
180.	A-180	*pièce esquillée*	sieve, lag sand.	
181.	A-181	AWF/SSF	sieve, lag sand.	
182.	A-182	BRF	sieve, soils.	
183.	A-183	AWF	sieve, soils	A-107.
184.	A-184	AWF	sieve, soils.	
185.	A-185	SSF	sieve, soils.	
186.	A-186	cutter (util. flake)	sieve, soils.	
187.	A-187	tool fragment	sieve, soils.	
188.	A-188	tool fragment	sieve, soils.	
189.	A-189	flake fragment	sieve, soils.	
190.	A-190	unidentified flake	sieve, soils.	
191.	A-191	flake fragment	sieve, soils.	
192.	A-192	BRF	sieve, soils.	
193.	A-193	--		
194.	A-194	flake fragment	sieve, soils.	
195.	A-195	flake fragment	sieve, soils.	
196.	A-196	BRF	sieve, soils.	
197.	A-197	tool fragment	sieve, soils.	
198.	A-198	AWF/SSF	sieve, soils.	
199.	A-199	AWF/SSF	sieve, soils.	
200.	A-200	AWF/SSF	sieve, soils.	
201.	A-201	*pièce esquillée*	sieve, soils.	
202.	A-202	*pièce esquillée*	sieve, soils.	
203.	A-203	AWF/SSF	sieve, soils.	
204.	A-204	URF	sieve, soils.	
205.	A-205	AWF/SSF	sieve, soils.	
206.	A-206	AWF/SSF	sieve, soils.	
207.	A-207	AWF/SSF	sieve, soils.	
208.	A-208	unidentified flake	sieve, soils.	
209.	A-209	BRF	sieve, soils.	
210.	A-210	URF	sieve, soils.	
211.	A-211	pot-lidded flake	sieve, soils.	
212.	A-212	URF	sieve, soils.	
213.	A-213	BRF	sieve, soils.	
214.	A-214	tool fragment	*in situ*, lag sand	A-43, A-102, A-214, A-288.
215.	A-215	AWF/SSF	*in situ*, lag sand.	
216.	A-216	cutter (micro-graver)	*in situ*, lag sand.	
217.	A-217	BRF	*in situ*, lag sand.	
218.	A-218	burin	*in situ*, lag sand.	
219.	A-219	AWF/SSF	*in situ*, soils.	
220.	A-220	BRF	*in situ*, soils.	
221.	A-221	URF	*in situ*, soils.	
222.	A-222	core	*in situ*, soils.	
223.	A-223	trianguloid endscraper	*in situ*, lag sand.	
224.	A-224	BRF	*in situ*, soils.	
225.	A-225	BRF	*in situ*, soils.	
226.	A-226	BRF	*in situ*, soils.	
227.	A-227	BRF	*in situ*, lag sand.	
228.	A-228	BRF	sieve, soils.	
229.	A-229	BRF	sieve, soils.	
230.	A-230	BRF	sieve, soils.	
231.	A-231	BRF	sieve, soils.	
232.	A-232	SSF	sieve, soils.	
233.	A-233	--		
234.	A-234	flake fragment	sieve, lag sand.	
235.	A-235	flake fragment	sieve, lag sand.	
236.	A-236	BRF	sieve, lag sand	A-69.
237.	A-237	flake fragment	sieve, lag sand.	

238.	A-238	cutter (flaked graver)	sieve, lag sand.	
239.	A-239	--		
240.	A-240	unidentified flake	sieve, lag sand.	
241.	A-241	*pièce esquillée*	sieve, lag sand.	
242.	A-242	--		
243.	A-243	cutter (util. flake)	*in situ,* lag sand.	
244.	A-244	flake fragment	sieve, lag sand.	
245.	A-245	cutter (util. flake)	sieve, lag sand.	
246.	A-246	*pièce esquillée*	*in situ,* soils.	
247.	A-247	tool fragment	sieve, lag sand.	
248.	A-248	trianguloid endscraper	sieve, lag sand.	
249.	A-249	BRF	sieve, lag sand.	
250.	A-250	BRF	sieve, lag sand.	
251.	A-251	AWF/SSF	sieve, lag sand.	
252.	A-252	AWF/SSF	sieve, lag sand.	
253.	A-253	--		
254.	A-254	AWF/SSF	sieve, lag sand.	
255.	A-255	unidentified flake	sieve, lag sand.	
256.	A-256	cutter (util. flake)	*in situ,* soils.	
257.	A-257	AWF/SSF	*in situ,* soils.	
258.	A-258	AWF/SSF	*in situ,* soils.	
259.	A-259	*pièce esquillée*	*in situ,* soils.	
260.	A-260	AWF/SSF	*in situ,* soils.	
261.	A-261	AWF/SSF	*in situ,* lag sand.	
262.	A-262	cutter (util. flake)	sieve, lag sand.	
263.	A-263	BRF	sieve, soils.	
264.	A-264	BRF	*in situ,* soils.	
265.	A-265	tool fragment	sieve, lag sand.	
266.	A-266	unidentified flake	sieve, lag sand.	
267.	A-267	URF	sieve, lag sand.	
268.	A-268	BRF	sieve, lag sand.	
269.	A-269	*pièce esquillée*	*in situ,* soils.	
270.	A-270	cutter (util. flake)	*in situ,* soils.	
271.	A-271	trianguloid endscraper	*in situ,* lag sand.	
272.	A-272	--		
273.	A-273	cutter (util. flake)	*in situ,* lag sand.	
274.	A-274	trianguloid endscraper	*in situ,* lag sand.	
275.	A-275	tool fragment	*in situ,* lag sand.	
276.	A-276	AWF/SSF	*in situ,* lag sand.	
277.	A-277	trianguloid endscraper	*in situ,* lag sand.	
278.	A-278	tool fragment	sieve, soils.	
279.	A-279	*pièce esquillée*	sieve, soils.	
280.	A-280	AWF/SSF	sieve, soils.	
281.	A-281	AWF/SSF	sieve, soils.	
282.	A-282	trianguloid endscraper	sieve, soils.	
283.	A-283	cutter (micro-graver)	*in situ,* soils.	
284.	A-284	flake fragment	sieve, lag sand.	
285.	A-285	BRF	sieve, lag sand.	
286.	A-286	BRF	sieve, lag sand.	
287.	A-287	flake fragment	sieve, lag sand.	
288.	A-288	*pièce esquillée*	sieve, lag sand	A-43, A-102, A-208, A-214.
289.	A-289	unidentified flake	*in situ,* soils.	
290.	A-290	tool fragment	*in situ,* lag sand.	
291.	A-291	AWF/SSF	*in situ,* lag sand	A-98.
292.	A-292	unidentified flake	sieve, backdirt.	
293.	A-293	cutter (util. flake)	sieve, backdirt.	
294.	A-293A	unidentified flake fragment	sieve, backdirt.	
295.	A-294	AWF	sieve, backdirt.	
296.	A-295	flake fragment	sieve, backdirt.	
297.	A-296	flake fragment	sieve, backdirt.	
298.	A-297	unidentified flake	sieve, backdirt.	
299.	A-298	BRF fragment	sieve, backdirt	A-66.
300.	A-299	flake fragment	sieve, backdirt.	

301.	A-300	BRF	sieve, backdirt.
302.	A-301	flake fragment	sieve, backdirt.
303.	A-302	flake fragment	sieve, backdirt.
304.	A-303	AWF/SSF	sieve, backdirt.
305.	A-304	cutter (util. flake)	sieve, backdirt.
306.	A-305	AWF/SSF	sieve, backdirt.
307.	A-306	cutter (util. flake)	sieve, backdirt.
308.	A-307	flake fragment	sieve, backdirt.
309.	A-308	flake fragment	sieve, backdirt.
310.	A-309	URF	sieve, backdirt.
311.	A-310	BRF	sieve, backdirt.
312.	A-311	cutter (util. flake)	sieve, backdirt.
313.	A-312	AWF/SSF	sieve, backdirt.
314.	A-313	unidentified flake	sieve, backdirt.
315.	A-314	unidentified flake	sieve, backdirt.
316.	A-315	*pièce esquillée*	sieve, backdirt.
317.	A-316	AWF/SSF	sieve, backdirt.
318.	A-317	BRF	sieve, backdirt A-1, A-2, A-50, A-55, A-78, A-169
319.	A-318	URF	sieve, backdirt.
320.	A-319	trianguloid endscraper	sieve, backdirt.
321.	A-320	URF	sieve, backdirt.
322.	A-321	AWF/SSF	sieve, backdirt.
323.	A-322	AWF/SSF	sieve, backdirt.
324.	A-323	unidentified flake	sieve, backdirt.
325.	A-324	BRF	sieve, backdirt.
326.	A-325	BRF	sieve, backdirt.
327.	A-326	AWF/SSF	sieve, backdirt.
328.	A-327	AWF/SSF	sieve, backdirt.
329.	A-328	BRF	sieve, backdirt.
330.	A-329	AWF/SSF	sieve, backdirt.
331.	A-330	BRF	sieve, backdirt.
332.	A-331	AWF/SSF	sieve, backdirt.
333.	A-332	AWF/SSF	sieve, backdirt.
334.	A-333	cutter (util. flake)	sieve, backdirt.
335.	A-334	AWF/SSF	sieve, backdirt.
336.	A-335	unidentified flake	sieve, backdirt.
337.	A-336	AWF/SSF	sieve, backdirt.
338.	A-337	unidentified flake	sieve, backdirt.
339.	A-338	cutter (util. flake)	sieve, backdirt.
340.	A-339	cutter (util. flake)	sieve, backdirt.
341.	A-340	AWF/SSF	sieve, backdirt.
342.	A-341	unidentified flake	sieve, backdirt.
343.	A-342	AWF/SSF	sieve, backdirt.
344.	A-343	BRF	sieve, backdirt.
345.	A-344	unidentified flake	sieve, backdirt.
346.	A-345	BRF	sieve, backdirt.
347.	A-346	cutter (util. flake)	sieve, backdirt.
348.	A-347	AWF/SSF	sieve, backdirt.
349.	A-348	AWF/SSF	sieve, backdirt.
350.	A-349	flake fragment	sieve, backdirt.
351.	A-350	BRF	sieve, backdirt.
352.	A-351	BRF	sieve, backdirt.
353.	A-352	BRF	sieve, backdirt.
354.	A-353	cutter (micro-graver)	sieve, backdirt.
355.	A-354	SSF	sieve, backdirt.
356.	A-355	unidentified flake	sieve, backdirt.
357.	A-356	BRF	sieve, backdirt.
358.	A-357	URF	sieve, backdirt.
359.	A-358	AWF/SSF	sieve, backdirt.
360.	A-359	SSF	sieve, backdirt.
361.	A-360	unidentified flake	sieve, backdirt.
362.	A-361	tool fragment	sieve, backdirt.

363. A-362	*pièce esquillée*	sieve, backdirt.	
364. A-363	SSF	sieve, backdirt.	
365. A-364	unidentified flake	sieve, backdirt.	
366. A-365	SSF	sieve, backdirt.	
367. A-366	tool fragment	sieve, backdirt.	
368. A-367	SSF	sieve, backdirt.	
369. A-368	URF	sieve, backdirt.	
370. A-369	SSF	sieve, backdirt.	
371. A-370	BRF	sieve, backdirt.	
372. A-371	SSF	sieve, backdirt.	
373. A-372	BRF	sieve, backdirt.	
374. A-373	SSF	sieve, backdirt.	
375. A-374	sidescraper fragment	sieve, backdirt	A-5, A-27.
376. A-375	unidentified flake	sieve, backdirt.	
377. A-376	SSF	sieve, backdirt.	
378. A-377	SSF	sieve, backdirt.	
379. A-378	SSF	sieve, backdirt.	
380. A-379	SSF	sieve, backdirt.	
381. A-380	SSF	sieve, backdirt.	
382. A-381	burin	sieve, backdirt.	
383. A-382	unidentified flake	sieve, backdirt.	
384. A-383	BRF	sieve, backdirt.	
385. A-384	---		
386. A-385	URF	sieve, backdirt.	
387. A-386	unidentified flake	sieve, backdirt.	
388. A-387	SSF	sieve, backdirt.	
389. A-388	SSF	sieve, backdirt.	
390. A-389	URF	sieve, backdirt.	
391. A-390	SSF	sieve, backdirt.	
392. A-391	URF	sieve, backdirt.	
393. A-392	SSF	sieve, backdirt.	
394. A-393	URF	sieve, backdirt.	
395. A-394	unidentified flake	sieve, backdirt.	
396. A-395	SSF	sieve, backdirt.	
397. A-396	SSF	sieve, backdirt.	
398. A-397	BRF	sieve, backdirt.	
399. A-398	SSF	sieve, backdirt.	
400. A-399	URF	sieve, backdirt.	
401. A-400	SSF	sieve, backdirt.	
402. A-401	URF	sieve, backdirt.	
403. A-402	URF	sieve, backdirt.	
404. A-403	URF	sieve, backdirt.	
405. A-404	flake fragment	sieve, backdirt.	
406. A-405	unidentified flake	sieve, backdirt.	
407. A-406	---		
408. A-407	BRF	*in situ,* soils.	
409. A-408	BRF	*in situ,* soils.	
410. A-409	AWF	*in situ,* soils.	
411. A-410	cutter (util. flake)	*in situ,* soils.	
412. A-411	*pièce esquillée*	*in situ,* soils.	
413. A-412	unidentified flake	*in situ,* soils.	
414. A-413	SSF	*in situ,* soils.	
415. A-414	URF	*in situ,* soils.	
416. A-415	tool fragment	*in situ,* soils.	
417. A-416	URF	*in situ,* soils.	
418. A-417	BRF	*in situ,* soils.	
419. A-418	URF	*in situ,* soils.	
420. A-419	flake fragment	*in situ,* soils.	
421. A-420	URF	unknown findspot.	
422. A-421	flake fragment	unknown findspot.	
423. A-422	BRF	sieve, lag sand.	
424. A-423	trianguloid endscraper	sieve, lag sand.	
425. A-424	trianguloid endscraper	sieve, lag sand.	

118

426.	A-425	*pièce esquillée*	sieve, lag sand.
427.	A-426	trianguloid endscraper	sieve, lag sand.
428.	A-427	trianguloid endscraper	*in situ,* soils.
429.	A-428	trianguloid endscraper	sieve, lag sand.
430.	A-429	trianguloid endscraper	sieve, lag sand.
431.	A-430	*pièce esquillée*	*in situ,* lag sand.
432.	A-431	trianguloid endscraper	*in situ,* soils.
433.	A-432	BRF	sieve, lag sand A-440.
434.	A-433	BRF	sieve, lag sand.
435.	A-434	AWF	sieve, lag sand.
436.	A-435	AWF	*in situ,* lag sand.
437.	A-436	SSF	*in situ,* lag sand.
438.	A-437	SSF	*in situ,* lag sand.
439.	A-438	tool fragment	sieve soils.
440.	A-439	*pièce esquillée*	sieve, soils.
441.	A-440	flake fragment	sieve, lag sand A-432.
442.	A-441	tool fragment	*in situ,* soils.
443.	A-442	sidescraper	*in situ,* soils.
444.	A-443	sidescraper	sieve, lag sand.
445.	A-444	BRF	*in situ,* soils A-445, A-421.
446.	A-445	flake fragment	*in situ,* soils A-444, A-421.
447.	A-446	*pièce esquillée*	sieve, lag sand.
448.	A-447	unidentified flake	sieve, soils.
449.	A-448	BRF	sieve, lag sand.
450.	A-449	flake fragment	sieve, soils.
451.	A-450	SSF	sieve, soils.

*BRF = biface reduction flake   SSF = scaled or splintered flake

AWF = angular waste flake   URF = uniface resharpening flake